# Simplified Fly Fishing

# SIMPLIFIED

*It gets you
on the water
and fishing with flies
in half an hour*

STACKPOLE BOOKS

# FLY FISHING

## by S. R. Slaymaker II

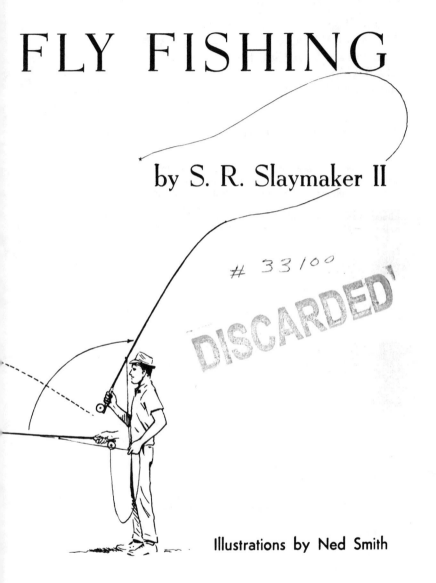

Illustrations by Ned Smith

Published by
STACKPOLE BOOKS
Cameron and Kelker Streets
P.O. Box 1831
Harrisburg, PA 17105

*Original hardcover edition published in 1969.*

Printed in the United States of America

10 9 8 7 6 5 4 3 2 1

**Library of Congress Cataloging-in-Publication Data**

Slaymaker, S. R.
    Simplified fly fishing.

    Includes index.
    1. Fly fishing.   I. Title.
SH451.S59     1988          799.1'2          87-7088
ISBN 0-8117-2279-1

# Contents

More's the pity that fly fishing is widely considered an elitist pastime rather than what it really is: an easy-to-learn tool of gamefish conservation that needs more converts.

This book is dedicated to Lefty Kreh and Gardner Grant, who tirelessly use their diverse and considerable talents in spreading the truth about fly fishing.

Sam Slaymaker

# Foreword

I've never met an angler competent in many areas of angling who didn't say that when conditions are right, fly fishing is more fun than anything else. This opinion is shared by anglers as varied as business tycoons who battle giant tuna from their own fishing machines to the many fishermen who simply enjoy catching bluegills. Fly fishing is fun—even the casting is a joy. It's something similar to target shooting, but you get your "bullets" back with each backcast. In short, if you want to get the most fun possible from fishing, try it with a fly rod.

Only rather recently have many experts been conveying the message that fly fishing is an easy sport to start and that it offers a long, fun-filled road to mastery. Not too long ago, titans of the sport led most of us to believe that only if you had been touched by the hand of God would you ever be able to fish well with a fly rod. That view was hogwash, and many participants deplored it.

One of the best debunkers of this elitist line of thought was Sam Slaymaker, who in the 1960s wrote *Simplified Fly*

*Fishing.* I read it, embraced it, and thought, "Here's something I can recommend with enthusiasm to people who want to get involved in the sport and know nothing of it." Naturally, a serious beginner would still need to read other books and get casting practice plus on-the-stream work. But Sam's book was a solid first step toward mastery of this fascinating sport.

*Simplified Fly Fishing* was widely read in the late 1960s and 70s, but the hardcover edition has been out of print for several years. Since the numbers of beginners and fly-fishing converts grow so rapidly, there is a continuing need for this little classic. I'm thankful that Stackpole is bringing it out in this softcover edition.

I firmly believe that *Simplified Fly Fishing* was instrumental in helping to create the boom in fly fishing that began in the early 1970s. One big reason for the book's success was Sam Slaymaker's recommendation of training areas: farm ponds. Many people considered this a stroke of genius because a key step for beginning fly rodders is the gaining of confidence.

What could be simpler than learning with easy-to-catch bluegills and bass on obstacle-free, easy-to-fish farm ponds? In a very short time, the beginner gains confidence and is hooked on fly fishing for life. Sam's ideas on how to fish a farm pond are also useful because they allow the novice angler to test what he has read without having anyone else watch.

Sam gives clear and concise instructions on how to go about finding and preparing to fish farm ponds. Then he gets into the more sophisticated trout, but not at first on streams. He recommends pay-to-fish trout ponds. By the time Sam gets the reader on a proper trout stream, most of his beginner difficulties will be ironed out.

Many of today's writers are so complex in their approach to fly fishing that newcomers will be frightened into thinking you need a degree in entomology to catch a trout. Sam's easy-to-follow, solid, and effective steps on coping with fly-imitation and stream problems are excellent.

In some books, instructions on nymph fishing for trout are complicated. Sam avoids this hazard by treating wet flies and nymphs as the same thing. And he recommends fishing them (when possible) upstream—a forerunner of today's "emerger" patterns.

If you read this book carefully, you should have a good idea of where the fish will be in the stream and why. After a thorough study of these pages, you should be able to step into the right water, with the proper leader and fly, and have some measure of understanding and confidence in how to catch that fish.

The book is also of value to experienced fly fishers, thanks to an interesting and informative chapter on the collecting of a fly angler's library. It has been up-dated and expanded for this new edition.

*Simplified Fly Fishing*, I'm sure, is the book that experts in the field will be recommending for a long time to come to people starting in the wonderful world of fly fishing.

Lefty Kreh

# Acknowledgments

A writer whose book includes a foreword by Lefty Kreh is like the proverbial tail that wags the dog; this writer is more than happy to have it that way.

For authorizing use of its Moviegram, "Lessons in Fly Casting," a debt of gratitude is owed the Weber Tackle Company of Stevens Point, Wisconsin.

My thanks also go to my long-suffering typist wife, Sally.

# Introduction

This book is written primarily for non-fishermen who want to learn to fly fish, for bait fishermen who have put off switching to flies because of the common but erroneous belief that they are for experts only, and for some-time fly anglers seeking simple but effective tips with which to improve their techniques. Excellent how-to books on the subject have been written, but few demonstrate that fly angling is one of the simplest of all pastimes to master. This I have tried to prove by showing how those who have never held a fishing rod can become fly fishermen in minutes. The following is a novel treatment of the four phases of fly angling; the fishing of streamers, wet flies, nymphs, and dry flies—the purpose being to show how skill with artificial flies can be quickly acquired by anyone, that it need not necessarily represent the fruits of years astream.

Many are persuaded that a book of this kind is especially timely. For growing numbers of fishermen—particularly those interested in trout—are being forced to fish with flies. Dissatisfaction with put-and-take trout-stocking programs of most states is becoming widespread. Its hallmarks—fishermen staking out recently planted fish by tailing hatchery trucks, "Opening Day" with its carnival-like atmosphere, the preoccupation of state public relations officials with "limit" catches —are as unsportsmanlike as they are unsound in terms of conservation. The reaction of true trout conservationists is the espousal of a new concept—"natural angling," the seeking of a given species of game fish, in its proper habitat, with tackle which permits fish to perform to capacity.

For trout this rules out worms and live bait. Unlike artificial flies, the former are easily swallowed by fish and their fighting ability is reduced. More important, deep hooking often injures and kills fish; they cannot be returned to the water and caught again. What with exploding populations and ever diminishing water resources, it is mandatory that trout be used more than once. Then the enjoyment of catching them in the most sporting manner can be experienced by a rapidly expanding number of anglers.

By way of providing sufficient trout in their natural environment, there has been a phenomenal expansion of "fly fish only" and "catch and release" streams in state and federal parks and forests. Remaining trout water is quickly being acquired by clubs, and here, too, economy usually dictates "flies only." Thus the bait fisherman in quest of trout will be so increasingly hedged in that eventually he will be forced to flies in self-defense.

Even if such compelling reasons for fishing flies did not exist, all fishermen should do so because they make for infinitely more thrills. The light weight of a fly rod magnifies that of the fish; its whippiness permits the fish more leeway for fighting. Optimum action results.

Our aim will be to fish together through these pages, toward the end of learning through doing. No matter how you may categorize yourself with respect to skill, I hope that the experience will prove rewarding toward helping you to improve it—thereby increasing your enjoyment of the delightful art form that is fly angling.

S. R. Slaymaker II
"White Chimneys"
Gap, Pennsylvania

# CHAPTER 1

# How to Take Your First Fish on a Fly...in One Evening!

You can become a fly angler in about thirty minutes. I've been saying this to bait fishermen and the complete beginner for many years, and invariably the answer is a disbelieving laugh. But when given a chance, I can prove it, to each doubting Thomas. Most equate fly angling with hard-to-reach mountain streams, intricate and expensive equipment, and skill that's inborn. As we shall see, they are wrong on all counts.

Unless you live in the heart of one of the largest metropolitan areas in the U.S.A., chances are very good that you're only an hour or less from prime fly-fishing water—farm ponds teaming with scrappy bluegill, sunfish, and hard-fighting largemouth bass. Farm ponds are easy to find and readily accessible; rural communities are girded by them. The urban sprawl has even placed many in big-city suburbs. According to the U.S. Department of the Interior's Fish and Wildlife Service, there are over 1,500,000 private reservoirs of under ten acres, the vast majority of which are stocked by the Service with bass and bluegills. Surprisingly, most farm ponds are very lightly fished. Proof that pond owners welcome fishermen is evident in a report by the Service revealing that 32 percent of all farm ponds are accessible to the public and that a larger number may be fished by requesting permission of the owner. So all you have to do is ask.

Generally unrealized, too, is the tremendous boon that farm ponds provide the beginning fly fisherman. Shallow and placid, these artificial impoundments make perfect training water, for they present none of the natural obstacles common to creeks, rivers, and larger lakes. Troublesome snagging, then, is eliminated. Since bluegills are so quick to strike, fledgling fly fishers are soon able to develop enough skill with artificial flies to catch the more highly prized largemouth bass. And, should a beginner be at all self-conscious, he is virtually assured of privacy on private water. But before visiting your first farm pond, a brief description of elementary tackle is in order.

Perhaps you have a fly rod. If so, use it no matter what the size. Should you not have one, a 7½-foot Fiberglas fly rod with medium action is ideal for beginning and for many, if not most occasions, throughout your angling life. Most leading rodmakers offer them. If your sporting goods store does not have any in stock, one can quickly be ordered.

Fly-rod reels range in size from less than 3 inches in diameter to more than 4 inches. Pick one with single action of 3¼ inches in diameter.

It is very important that your line match the rod. A size D floating line (level) will meet your requirements for the time being. You will note that fly line is much thicker and heavier than ordinary bait-casting line or spin-casting monofilament. This precludes attaching flies directly to the line; a nylon leader tied to the line makes it possible to affix the fly. Also, the gossamer leader is harder for fish to detect than the much heavier line. The leader, then, keeps the line out of the fish's view. You should ask for several 4-foot bugging leaders with no taper, 3.5-pound test. Extras are handy in the event of breaking or knotting.

For your immediate purpose a half dozen of any kind of artificial flies will do. Whether they are trout flies or bass bugs or wet flies, dries or nymphs or even plastic creations makes little difference. They should, however, be tied on small hooks, preferably nothing larger than a No. 10. Buy fingernail clippers and you're ready to go. With a very modest outlay you are ready to begin your career as a fly fisherman. Remember that the rod, representing the major amount of your purchase, will serve you for years, possibly for life.

Farm-pond bluegills and bass feed most actively during long windless summer evenings. No longer vexed by bankside tremors caused by farm machinery and animals, many haunt shallows for smaller fish, tiny tadpoles, and frogs. Others rise from cool depths, where the sun's blaze had driven them earlier, and now they hover near a glassy surface awaiting hatching flies, or falling flies and insects whose undulating descent through the soft afterglow is described by the crazy wheeling of hungry swallows. The stage is set for action.

So your first pond-prospecting trip should be timed for arrival in a rural or semirural area by late afternoon. Thus there's sufficient opportunity to scout for farms with ponds. Also, on finding one, you will have to set up your rig—after unhurried amenities with the landowner. Ask him if his pond is stocked with bluegills and bass. Nine times out of ten it will be. Then mention your desire to learn to fly fish. Comment on how the privacy of his pond affords ideal training water, as opposed, say, to crowded public water. You might add that you will return any catches should he want you to. Be sure to stress that this can be done safely when flies are used, as fish

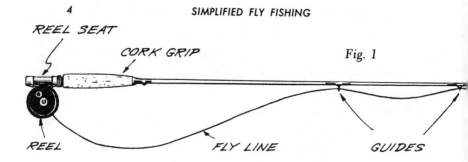

REEL SEAT

CORK GRIP

Fig. 1

REEL        FLY LINE        GUIDES

rarely swallow them like live bait. Sometimes a proffered dollar bill helps, but it is rarely necessary. The vast majority of pond owners will ask you in and tell you to keep what you catch. If your luck is good, however, a few fish for his pan are often appreciated. Above all, assure him that you will respect his premises. The only pond I had trouble getting on was one on which a fisherman had worn out his welcome by constant littering.

Now assemble the gear and familiarize yourself with its potential. Your rod will come in two pieces. Insert the tip end in the hollow section of the butt piece (the ferrule). Be sure to keep the line guides on both rod sections evenly aligned so that line will slide smoothly along the entire rod. Push, don't twist, the sections together.

Then tie an end of your line to the spool in the center of your reel. With the clippers, trim ends protruding from the knot. So as not to kink or tangle line, crank the reel handle slowly until all line is transferred to the reel as the coil is rotated.

Now place the reel in the reel seat to the rear of your rod's handle and fasten it with the sliding ring on the reel seat. When you grip your rod, the reel should be suspended below it. Disregarding the little eyelet on the base of the rod's butt section (it's for attaching the fly when not in use), string the line through the rod guides. After it has passed through the

FERRULE

TIP-TOP

LEADER

end guide, knot it to the leader's looped end. For the time being, use whatever knot you find easiest to tie. This particular leader is so short that line retrieving will not dictate bringing the leader through the top guides, as would be the case with a longer trout leader. Here the nail knot is helpful, and along with others, it will be described later. Before attaching a fly, let's discover what your fly rod is supposed to do (Fig. 1).

If you have fished with (or watched others use) bait-casting or spinning rigs, it is immediately obvious that line is pulled from the reel by the heavier bait when it is thrown or cast. Featherweight flies cannot propel the heavier line, so fly casting is different. It is really line casting, as it is your line which has the necessary weight to be carried through the air like a spinning or bait-casting lure. The whipping action of your rod powers the line which, in turn, carries the lure.

Your reel, then, cannot be used like a bait-casting or spinning reel. For the fly line and lure are not so heavy as to activate it and cause it to feed out line when it is cast. So, unlike other reels, which do deliver line (thanks to the heavier lure) and take it back again on the retrieve, fly-rod reels are simply storehouses for line. Line to be cast is stripped from the reel with one hand while you hold the rod in the other. Slide line ahead of you from the water into the air behind. Pause, then bring the rod forward. Near the end of the forward whip of the rod, release line in your hand. Retrieve line simply by pulling it in with your line hand. Slack line is held in coils or dropped at your feet until it is cast again.

Now grip the cork handle of the rod in your right hand (if you're right-handed; reverse if you're a lefty) and try some practice casts—on the grass beside the pond, without a fly. Make sure that the end of the leader is free of all the rod guides and that about 20 feet of line is stretched out ahead of you on the grass (Fig. 2). Strip about 5 feet of line from the reel and let it drop at your feet. Holding the uppermost portion of the slack line tightly, raise the rod tip, lifting line from the ground (Fig. 3). With a gradually accelerated motion, swift enough to throw the line into the air behind you, whip your rod back. Pause long enough to permit the line, now to your rear, to straighten out. Before it touches ground, flick the rod forward again with gradually accelerated motion and simultaneously release the slack line in your left hand. The 20 feet of line in the air will sail forward, carrying the extra 5 feet of slack along. You will have made a cast, then, of about 25 feet. Twenty- to 35-foot casts are standard under most fly-fishing conditions.

That is the basic procedure in fly casting. You need only the rig you have and two hands. Disregard the expert who regales you with long lectures on arm positioning and wrist action; with practice you will develop skill, making one motion blend into the next. By way of developing proper timing, the simplified Moviegram method of casting in Chapter 3 will be helpful, but for now try more practice casts on the grass. Your first few tries were probably too jerky. Remember, keep the line in the air from the time you lift it from the ground until your cast is completed. This is easier to accomplish when you handle a minimum amount of line, so don't practice with any more than 15 to 20 feet, laid out, and that extra 5 feet of

*Fig.* 2

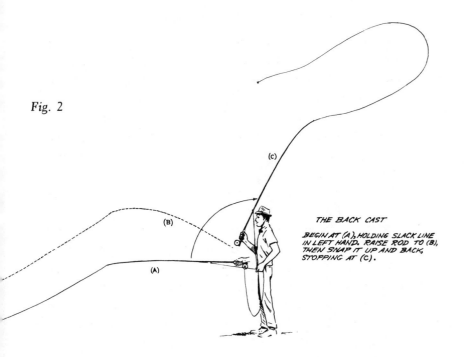

THE BACK CAST

BEGIN AT (A), HOLDING SLACK LINE
IN LEFT HAND. RAISE ROD TO (B),
THEN SNAP IT UP AND BACK,
STOPPING AT (C).

*Fig.* 3

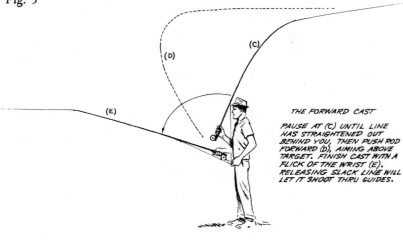

THE FORWARD CAST

PAUSE AT (C) UNTIL LINE
HAS STRAIGHTENED OUT
BEHIND YOU, THEN PUSH ROD
FORWARD (D), AIMING ABOVE
TARGET. FINISH CAST WITH A
FLICK OF THE WRIST (E).
RELEASING SLACK LINE WILL
LET IT SHOOT THRU GUIDES.

slack in hand. Just remember: pick up, whip back (but not long enough to let the line touch down behind you), whip forward and release your slack, all in a gradually accelerated motion. Remember, too, that the backward and forward movements of your rod must be smooth, not jerky. Practice on the grass until you can shoot your line, but don't expect to make accurate casts right away. So long as your line feeds out anywhere in the area ahead, you will be able to snag a bluegill.

Knot a fly to the end of the leader, and trim away excess leader with your nail clippers. After checking the rear for possible obstructions, face the pond, and toss the 20 feet of line on the water in front of you. Strip off the 5 feet of slack; hold it in your line hand; cast as before. On completing the cast, don't budge the fly for fifteen or twenty seconds. Then draw it in slowly with a hand-twist retrieve, and with short rod-tip jerks, coiling line in or around your line hand. Your fly should be on or just under the surface. You are simulating a fallen insect and its subsequent struggle in or on the water. No matter how realistic your fly looks to fish, it is the action that will attract. You will feel a breathtaking thrill when the wake of a fish knifes toward the fly. Often there's no take. He may be just looking it over, and if this happens, stop the retrieve. Let the fly drift for a few seconds, then continue again with short jerks. When leader approaches the tip guide, prepare to cast again. Now it's time to skid the fly from the water and throw it into a high back cast preparatory to the next delivery.

After fishing water dead ahead, cast several times slightly to the right, then to the left. When the area within covering distance is worked, move along the bank to unfished water. If you see a fish swirl at a natural insect, cast to him. Even if your fly is a couple of yards off target, there's a good chance that he will see its fall and take it. Rising fish are good prospects, for they're obviously on the make.

Sooner or later you will be rewarded. A flash of lavender-flecked red-orange, coupled with a gurgling splash, signals the strike of a bluegill. A quick upward flick of your rod should set the hook, but you will probably be too stunned to strike back. Chances are it won't matter; hard-hitting bluegills will usually hook themselves. The bare 2 ounces of the rod's weight will magnify the fish's weight, especially when he turns broadside and sets off on a long curving run.

Resist the urge to give with a mighty haul and lift the fish clear. Just keep the line taut and your rod tip high, and steadily retrieve line in your hand until the fish nears the bank. If you want to release him, you can often do so without touching him by gripping the forward part of the fly and shaking him loose. When this doesn't work, some anglers wet their hands (so as to lessen removal of fishes' protective slime; others don't feel that hand-wetting is necessary) and grasp them from underneath, holding them in the middle by thumb and forefinger. Guard against touching the prickly dorsal fin. When unhooking bass, you can hold them more easily by grasping the lower jaw with thumb and forefinger.

Should bankside casting yield little action, there's another method which is sure-fire—bankside trolling.

I hit on this method as a substitute for casting when instructing five- to eight-year-olds in fly fishing. My purpose was to enable them to hook fish without casting. This could wait until action had whetted their appetites for practice.

The children were taught to toss out their lines, pointing rods towards the pond and walking its perimeter, trolling their flies behind. When the flies slipped diagonally into the bank, the children were instructed in retrieving the line, preparatory to throwing it out again.

This is the simplest approach to lure presentation, and it worked. Scrappy bluegills struck with wild abandon. Of course, there were many misses, but these afforded instantaneous excitement, and the likely promise of more strikes that might result in a hooked fish. The children were kept in a high state of excitement, and you will be, too, for even the most jaded adult can't fail to thrill at the darting, plunging antics of a hooked bluegill, whose bright flanks can pump your featherweight rod with a vengeance that belies his small size.

In the evening (and in early morning, also a prime feeding period), walk-trolling rarely fails to produce. The reason: your fly is close to the shoreline most of the time, and this is where bass do their heavy feeding. In shallows it's easier for them to trap frogs, fish, and insects. You must remember, though, that footfalls along the bank can spook shore-hugging bass ahead, so tread softly, as far in from the bank as possible.

You won't get much casting practice, but engraved on your mind's eye for all time to come will be unclouded memories of a blur of olive-white, an echoing crash of white water surrounding a glistening bass, airborne in fading twilight. Even the dogged fight of the bluegill pales against those jolting high jumps of the largemouth. The average farm-pond size is 10 to 14 inches, but 2-footers of 5 and 6 pounds are not uncommon. Should you tangle with a granddaddy, try to contain yourself enough to give him as much line as he'll take. Then bring him in as far as he will let you. When he runs again, surrender line and so on until he tires enough for you to beach him by reaching down and picking him up by his lower jaw. This procedure is known as playing the fish.

It doesn't matter if trolling the bank robs you of casting

experience, for the resulting action will get you hooked on flies. Dissatisfaction with live bait—or the idea of it, if you've never used it—will set in. Eventually, casting will take care of itself, and in the meantime, you will have become a fly fisherman.

# CHAPTER 2

# How to Catch Your First Trout on a Fly

Your first experience with flies on a farm pond will prove infectious, but don't stick to one pond. Even though all farm impoundments look alike, catches in different locales will build confidence in your ability to take fish on flies. Should there be any lingering doubts about your ability to snag the more sophisticated trout on flies, additional pond experience will enable you to kick them. So keep practicing on ponds—even in your yard—until your pickup, back cast, and delivery blend into each other.

It would be well, too, if you mastered the false cast. This has several purposes, but at the moment we're only concerned with achieving fair accuracy and distance. You simply keep the fly in the air—during the back cast and forward—while estimating the distance of your cast. The extent of line going back and forth is controlled by your gathering it in, or stripping it from the reel. When the desired amount is in the air, drop the fly. The false cast will be useful in some situations covered in this chapter.

Equipment and tips on its use will be thoroughly covered in

Chapter 7. But brief mention of some few basic items, over and above rod and reel, must come here to facilitate your graduation to trout water. Since stream fishing covered in this chapter pertains to early spring when streams are full, chest-high waders are better than hip boots. Trout fishing is hiking, so it's not convenient to carry a tackle box, and fishing vests are designed to hold all of your on-stream equipment. Since beaching fish is more difficult in streams than in ponds, a landing net should be bought. A knife is sometimes useful, but your nail clippers will suffice for snipping line and leader. You will need a few split-shot sinkers, the smallest available. Trout are generally more wary than bluegills and bass, so your leader should be longer and finer. Ask for a few packs of 7½-

NYMPH
SIZE 12

WET FLY
SIZE 12

(ALL SHOWN ACTUAL SIZE)

Fig. 4

DRY FLY
SIZE 12

BUCKTAIL STREAMER
SIZE 8 - 3X LONG

foot nylon trout leader, tapered to size 4 or 5X. Also, pick up a small pair of pliers. You should shop at a recognized sporting goods store with help competent enough to guide your purchases.

This additional equipment (with flies coming next) will not be expensive. Like the rod and reel, the bulk of these items will last for years, so contrary to popular belief, fly fishing does not have to be a very costly hobby.

The method we will first adopt requires several streamer flies, a few nymphs, as well as wet and dry flies (Fig. 4). Flies and nymphs should be dark in color, sizes 10 or 12. Artificial nymphs resemble unhatched underwater insects; wet flies simulate insects in the metamorphosis of hatching or adult flies, swamped underwater. Dry flies represent mature flies on the surface. Tied on long shank hooks (sizes 6 or 8), streamer flies are not meant to imitate fly life, as the name suggests, but small fish. They appeal to the cannibalistic instinct of trout and other game fish. You will need brightly colored streamers such as the Mickey Finn, Gray Ghost, Parmachene Belle, and Little Rainbow Trout.

### TROUT PONDS

In parts of the country with water cold enough to support trout (at least 70 degrees, as opposed to 75 degrees for bass and other warm-water species) there are growing numbers of pay-to-fish trout ponds. Your local newspaper's outdoor columnist or a sporting goods dealer will probably be able to direct you to one. Should a trout pond be nearby, taking your first trout on a fly will be almost as easy as catching your first bluegill or bass from a farm pond, for the basic method is the same. As before, you will be fishing from the bank, so boots won't be necessary. The only difference in the tackle used will be the longer trout leader and the flies mentioned before. In presentation there is also a slight variation: the nymph will be fished as deeply as possible, and its retrieve will be very slow. This might seem odd, for many have a calendar-art conception of trout—airborne, arching over surface flies. You will sometimes find this to be a true enough tableau, but it is a fact that trout feed underwater about 75 percent of the time. Their main fare is fly life in its nymphal stage, before they float surfaceward and fly away as mature flies. Nymphs mature on the bottom, in gravel, on sticks, and under and around rocks. Since they move sluggishly, when at all, they can often be easy prey for trout, so artificial nymphs are deadly when fished deep and slowly. Like farm ponds, man-made trout ponds have smooth bottoms and chances of snagging are nil.

To further fast sinking, using your pliers clamp a shot sinker on the leader in front of the nymph. Most fly anglers dislike lead as it makes casting awkward, but for deep-down pond trouting it's helpful. Later we will cover more convenient methods of weighting. Give your nymph plenty of time to sink; since the retrieving action is so slow, trout need not strike fast, and their takes may be so leisurely as to seem barely noticeable. There will be a slight bump, or a tightening of your line, as if it were snagged, but it can't be as this is not a natural obstacle-riddled bottom. It has to be a trout. So strike with a light upward lift of your rod. Too hard a strike will break the leader, or it might pull the lure from the trout's lips, which are possibly only nudging it. Your rod will snap to a quivering arch. If it's a rainbow trout, you can expect some acrobatics; a brown trout, too, will often jump clear of the water. The brawling brook trout will confine his action to diving runs, punctuated by vicious surface slashing. No matter which of these three major species of trout takes the nymph, the performance will be dramatic, thanks to your sensitive whiplike fly rod, plus in-the-mouth hooking, which gives these hard-fighting fish full latitude for action.

Play and land him exactly as you did bluegills or bass, like a large bass if he's heavy enough to run line from your reel. Remember not to horse him. When he seems ready, just drift him in head first.

Those who have worm fished for trout will probably note a striking similarity between their usual method and this one. For worm fishermen often confine their activity to deep pools full of stocked trout. Fat nightcrawlers are sunk to the bottom, though it is true that they're usually left lying for bites, and not retrieved for strikes.

All of which makes this particular nymph technique little more sporting than worm dunking. But it does prove that the nymph is not only as easy to fish as a worm, but that it is as effective as well. Even more so, particularly over these recently stocked pond trout, yet the vast majority of those who shy away from flies find this hard to believe.

Even beginning fly fishermen who find it hard to kick the worm-dunking habit can use nymphs as effectively as they once used worms. One nymph sunk to the bottom of a hole and lifted slowly is sheer murder on unsophisticated refugees from the hatchery.

Wet flies should be fished like nymphs—but higher up— since they are imitating a fly nearing the surface to hatch or, as noted, one that's been swamped in agitated water. A little jerking action should be added, though, since the natural fly struggles to get on the surface and shed his protective shuck.

For various reasons to be discussed later, dry flies are usually not as effective for trout on still water as are nymphs and wet flies. Still, when pond trout are surface feeding on a hatch of flies, you can often experience the height of angling thrills: that calendar view of a sparkling trout catapulting out of water and down, his gaping mouth aimed straight at your fly.

Examine the dry fly in Figure 4. You will note that unlike wet flies, the feathers are bunched at right angles to the hook's shank so that fibers are flared around it in a 360-degree circle. This tie, as opposed to that of the wet fly, facilitates the dry fly's floating. When these fibers are well soaked, however, the fly will begin to sink; to keep it dry, use the false cast. The whipping action in the air dries it out. Other methods of keeping dry flies dry will be taken up in Chapter 6.

You will probably wonder why we settled on dull-colored flies and bright streamers. The answer is simply that trout are rarely confronted with garish nymphs or flies. Most are brown or gray, and the majority of adult flies, whether lightly shaded or dark, are not bright. Our purpose, of course, is to deceive trout with realistic imitations of flies.

But the killer and cannibalistic instinct in game fish can often be aroused by bright colors, and this is particularly true with lures resembling and moving like smaller fish or minnows. The streamer, in simulating food fish, also attracts. Later we will learn the whens, whys, and wheres of the duller colored streamers, but the important thing now is the fact that we're fishing over unsophisticated hatchery fish. While they are fooled by something resembling natural food, they can also be easily attracted by the minnowlike darting of a colorful mass of fuzz and feathers.

Unless water is at its coldest, or warmest—both conditions are likely to put trout on the bottom—your streamer should be allowed to sink several feet below the surface, then retrieved in short jerks. A streamer strike is uncommonly vicious. The trout must be quick, lest the darting minnow escape him.

The four lures mentioned above—nymphs, wet flies, dry

flies, and streamers—are basic to all trout fishing everywhere. Basic, too, are these techniques suggested for use at trout lakes and ponds. Use them and you're sure to prove to yourself that flies are as easy to use and as effective as worms and live bait, and infinitely more enjoyable.

STREAM FISHING

Once over that initial not-so-high hurdle—your first trout on a fly—you're ready for classic trout fishing. The changing character of mountain streams offer anglers tableaus of matchless splendor and trout a natural habitat. Here their wiles and ability to fight afford enjoyment far beyond that possible in ponds.

Actually, the stream method with which we will begin is little more sporting than that prescribed for trout ponds, but it will serve as the basis for future learning. Again, it will prove that you can take trout on flies, this time on proper trout water.

Ask your local newspaper outdoor editor or sporting goods dealer for directions to the nearest fish-for-fun or fly-fish-only trout stream. Rules for the former usually require the return to water of all catches; the latter often have regulations permitting the killing of a certain number. If there are no such specially regulated streams within a reasonable distance, ask about public trout water, stocked by the state.

You should fish the average stocked trout stream very early in the season, before most of the fish are caught or die off. Specially regulated streams usually constitute better trout water: conditions permitting natural reproduction and/or the carrying of trout from one season to the next. Usually they are stocked more often than unregulated water, but it pays to fish these early, too, for you can be sure of a heavier concentration of fish. Since fly hatching is not very prevalent during the season's first days, confine your lures to nymphs or wet flies and streamers, the same ones used on trout ponds. Boots or waders will be necessary for this outing; also a landing net.

My first recommendation is not to go out too early, particularly on Opening Day. Large crowds of hole squatters won't catch all of the fish in those first hours; rather, they will wake up many fish and flush them into areas other than the big pools, where most are usually dumped from the hatchery truck. Many trout will be in riffles and broken water to begin with. Between stocking and opening, such phenomena as rain squalls, predators, livestock, hikers, and the quest for food will cause some circulation of fish.

Get on the stream after daylight when fish begin to cruise. Start at the top of a given stretch and work downstream, using a streamer. Pick the brightest; it will be seen better by trout in April's high and roily water.

By sunup, squatters will have claimed the better bankside pools. Give them a wide berth so as not to disturb their water. Only wade to reach potential hot spots. There are many kinds: usually they are patches of water formed by current deflectors such as boulders, sunken logs, stumps, jutting banks, and gravel bars. Such obstructions are often invisible, but their breaking of the current is not. They will be immediately obvious when you think like a fish. Trout, like people, don't enjoy expending unnecessary effort, and in sheltered, current-free areas, they don't have to. Against and under deflectors they feel more secure against encroachments of predators. Current deflectors are ideal feeding stations in which trout lie, facing upstream. While partially or entirely hidden, a trout is able to take a long look at potential food, such as downstream-drifting nymphs, hatching flies, and darting minnows, or their counterfeit equivalents—your nymphs, wet flies, and streamers. You don't have to be a tournament caster to take trout from such spots. In fact, you don't even have to cast. For now, concentrate on pocket water only, usually formed by curving rock formations (Fig. 5).

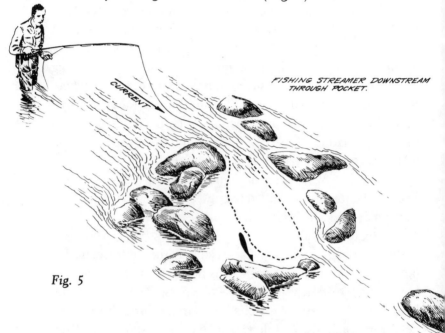

FISHING STREAMER DOWNSTREAM
THROUGH POCKET.

CURRENT

Fig. 5

Keeping your shadow off the water to be fished, sneak within several feet of the upstream side of one of those fishy-looking water pockets. Toss your streamer into it. As you retrieve against the current, slowly twitch the lure. You won't sample many such spots without getting a strike. Quick ones —so fast that you will miss some fish when you try to set the hook, for often trout will grab the hair or feathers only. When you miss, rest the pocket for a minute or two before flipping your streamer in again. I've counted as many as eleven passes at the same Mickey Finn by one stocked brookie. I nailed him on strike number twelve.

A flash of color and the instantaneous tug on your line that signals a near miss alerts you for the next pass, when you should vow to be ready for the fish. But should you miss again, there's always hope for another strike. And if none comes, there's doubtless another beautiful pocket just around the bend.

On all but the most jam-packed streams you will usually find these productive smaller spots unclaimed, even on Opening Day. Concentrate on them as far downstream as you care to go, but allow enough time for a return trip upstream. The same pockets, fished with the current instead of against it, will often yield splendid action. This time you will be fishing either

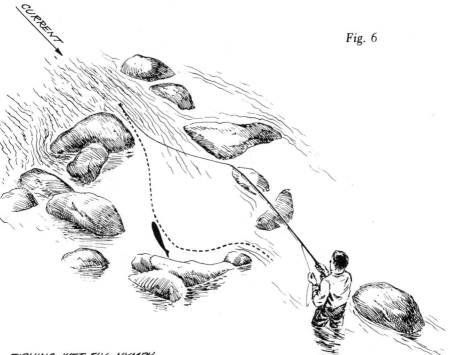

*Fig.* 6

FISHING WET FLY-NYMPH
UPSTREAM THROUGH POCKET.

a wet fly or a nymph, because while fish you spooked earlier can't as readily be attracted again by colorful streamers, they can often be deceived by the likes of a buggy morsel of food. And this is just what a dull-colored wet fly or nymph resembles as it tumbles near the bottom in a dead drift downstream.

This action is achieved by landing your fly in the upstream edges of pockets (Fig. 6). Casts will necessarily be short ones, as you should stand only 10 or 12 feet on the downstream side of the pocket. False casting will be helpful in estimating the amount of line needed, then deliver the fly as if you're on a pond. From the upstream edge, your fly will drift back naturally toward you. The pickup is made after it emerges at the pocket's downstream lip. No fly manipulation is necessary; the current does your work. Like a fly about to hatch—or one that's been swamped—your lure washes slowly into the trout's view. He senses that it's not about to get away, so he takes his time in picking it up. As on ponds, the result is a light bump, rather than a strike. Usually your only warning is a halt in the line's drift. A short quick upward flip of the wrist will set the hook.

The more cagey brown trout is less susceptible to the play of a colorful streamer than the carefree brookie and rainbow. This cautious trait seems bred even in hatchery browns, but bred in as well is a ravenous desire for fly life. So any dull-colored wet fly or nymph, presented realistically, can play havoc.

I proved this on a well-stocked but heavily fished mountain stream in western Pennsylvania, early in the 1965 season. Most of the big bankside pools were claimed, so I moved downstream, teasing a Little Brook Trout streamer into tempting-looking patches amid the riffles. In many there was the quick flash of a rainbow's crimson streak, or the rewarding pink-lavender blur in the amber depths that signaled the slashing take of a brookie.

An hour and a half of pocket hopping yielded six assorted rainbows and brooks. I kept four and then began my upstream trip with nymphs. After missing four or five deep-down nudges, I felt the thumping tug of a snagged brownie. The nicest fish of my entire day, this 14-incher went airborne three times before I was able to draw his head into the net. A total bag of four browns by upstream nymphing, plus the brooks and rainbows taken by downstream streamer flipping, demonstrated the efficiency of the different fly-fishing techniques.

Both are simple enough for the proverbial barefoot boy, and they will provide all the incentive you need to learn more about the four basic lures of the fly angler: the nymph, the wet fly, the dry fly, and the streamer.

But before beginning with streamers, since they are the easiest of fly-rod lures to use, your forward cast should be refined so that you can better cope with obstacles common to stream fishing.

# CHAPTER 3

# Casting, Playing, and Landing

The forward cast which you learned at the farm pond will suffice most of the time, wherever you fly fish. Now and again, though, you will meet situations requiring special casts. Before discussing them, however, it is vital that your forward cast be perfected by proper timing, the essence of effective fly casting. So this most basic of casts is reviewed in conjunction with Weber Tackle Company's simplified Moviegrams.

## TIMING THE ELEMENTARY PRACTICE CAST

While diagrams and directions apply to right-handed casters, lefties simply need to think in terms of the opposite hand.

Proper timing is easily achieved by practice casting in such a way that you view the line throughout the entire cycle of the cast. Note that in the drawing, the angler, facing the clock, is casting laterally, from left to right. While this is not a normal casting stance, it does enable him to keep watching his line's flight, back and forth.

After placing your rod on the ground with its tip pointing to

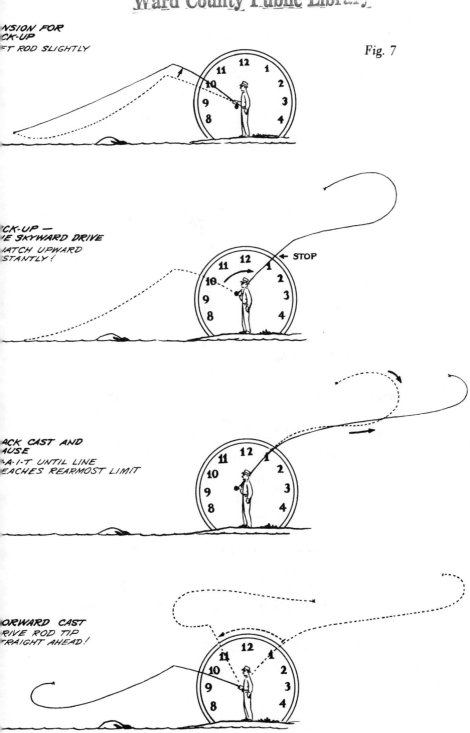

NSION FOR
CK-UP
T ROD SLIGHTLY

Fig. 7

11 12 1
10 2
9 3
8 4

CK-UP —
E SKYWARD DRIVE
ATCH UPWARD
STANTLY !

← STOP

11 12 1
10 2
9 3
8 4

ACK CAST AND
AUSE
A·I·T UNTIL LINE
EACHES REARMOST LIMIT

11 12 1
10 2
9 3
8 4

ORWARD CAST
RIVE ROD TIP
TRAIGHT AHEAD !

11 12 1
10 2
9 3
8 4

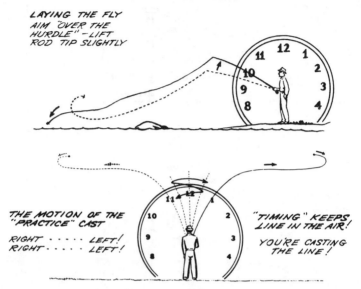

LAYING THE FLY
AIM "OVER THE
HURDLE" — LIFT
ROD TIP SLIGHTLY

THE MOTION OF THE
"PRACTICE" CAST

RIGHT · · · · · LEFT!
RIGHT · · · · · LEFT!

"TIMING" KEEPS
LINE IN THE AIR!

YOU'RE CASTING
THE LINE!

your left, lay out 20 to 30 feet of line and extend it straight out from the rod tip. Holding the line against the rod grip, raise the rod tip slowly to 10 o'clock. Then whip the tip upward with sufficient power to drive line smartly to your right. Stop the rod at 1 o'clock. Pause until the line reaches its entire extent, on your right, then, before it falls to the ground, briskly drive the rod tip to your left. Stop at 10 o'clock. Pause again until the line extends its length to your left, and repeat this left-right movement without allowing line to touch ground.

Observe your fly as it rides back and forth. Proper timing permits the line's movement to be smooth and your activating of it almost effortless. You will soon discover that a left or right drive that is too late or too soon causes improper timing and the falling of line to ground. Naturally, the extent of your pause between drives depends on the amount of line that is out. The more line that is in the air, the longer the pause so that it straightens out.

In facilitating proper timing of the elementary practice cast, it was recommended that line be held against the rod grip. Thus the handling of slack is unnecessary. After you feel that your timing is coming naturally, practice with slack in hand. Feed it out with your casts; retrieve it in sweeps, just as you did at the farm pond. Now, however, you will be learning line control with proper timing, and your casting will be smoother, and greater accuracy and distance will be achieved than was the case when you made your first casts with a fly rod.

When your sense of timing and line handling become involuntary, you can cast without observing the line's flight. Then assume the stance you take when actually fishing; turn sideways to the clock's face and cast over your shoulder. Note the accompanying diagrams.

TIMING THE FORWARD CAST

Now your line will be stretched out on the grass in front of you, as was the case when you began at the farm pond; 20 to 30 feet is sufficient. The rod tip is raised to 10 o'clock. This is high enough to remove slack from the line.

In a smooth action, jerk the tip upward so that the line reaches its full length to your rear. Then whip the tip forward. Exert the greatest force between 1 and 11 o'clock. Your rod should arrive at the horizontal position as the fly touches water. By way of making sure that your pause is correctly timed in the back cast, a quick glance to the rear might be helpful; but soon you will be able to sense when the line has reached its rearmost limit, and checking on it will be unnecessary.

The force which you impart to the rod comes from your forearm. Hold your elbow close to your side, pointing down. The wrist should be kept rigid, but not uncomfortably so.

Forearm action in the forward cast is not unlike that exerted when you're driving a nail into a wall. Hammer strokes are forward, not downward.

In order to cause the fly to light gently and before the leader, picture a 3-foot hurdle on your target area. As your cast nears completion, raise the rod tip enough to enable the fly to clear the hurdle.

## ROLL CASTING

When obstacles make a proper back cast difficult or impossible, the roll cast should be used. At least 30 feet of line must be laid out in front of you. Raise the rod backward, past your shoulder, to 1:30. Slack line will form a loop beside you. Exerting the greatest force between 1:30 and 11, snap the rod tip forward to 10 o'clock. Line will roll into a loop before you.

From the time that the loop forms at your side until the rod reaches the horizontal position motion must be smooth, not jerky; otherwise the fly will not follow the line's outward roll and light gently before it.

## SIDEARM CASTING

It's often necessary to angle your cast so that line won't get into the strike zone. The sidearm cast enables you to do this. It can also be used when obstructions overhead rule out forward casting. You will need 30 to 40 feet of clearance to your right or left. As this cast is really no more than the elementary practice cast executed horizontally rather than vertically. It's particularly easy to master because, like the practice cast, the line's ride is in plain view throughout the entire cycle of the cast.

There are other "obstacle casts" such as the bow and arrow cast and the steeple cast, not to mention the power or double haul cast, sometimes used against high winds, but these are seldom needed. The techniques covered here will take care of 95 percent of your time astream.

PLAYING AND LANDING

A principal obstacle to successful fish playing is the angler's nervous tension. With the strike, high excitement grips him, and even if he resists an urge to horse the fish, he's often hard put to take that all-important first step in playing—"feeling him out."

In boxing, when the first round begins, the cautious fighter throws out a feeler punch so as to anticipate the kind of fight his opponent will wage. This should be the intent of the cautious angler, in the first seconds after the fish's take. All too often though, the angler—particularly the beginning angler—is so fearful of losing his fish that he retrieves with his strike. Pressure added to that resulting from hook-setting is often enough to tear the hook from the fish's mouth; or, if he's a big one, to break the leader.

To continue the fight analogy, the opening bell is the fish's take; the first jab, light but sharp, is your hook-setting strike. The next step is to go on guard, allowing your adversary to maneuver. This is accomplished by exerting just enough pressure to keep the line taut; elimination of slack line helps to keep the hook set, but the pressure is light enough to permit the fish to run. As soon as he does, size him up so as to determine how much running need be allowed. In shallow trout streams you can often get a good look at him. When—as is often the case in lakes or deep pools—the take is so deep as to preclude your spotting the fish, size him up blind. Simply free your reel. If he can't turn it, chances are he's small enough to permit a cautious, even retrieve. If he runs your reel, he'll probably go 12 inches or over, so let him run. When he stops, exert a slight pressure in your direction until he takes off again, then surrender line. Always keep a taut line by exerting a light but steady pressure. This will tire him. Runs will become shorter, usually more circular, and he will begin to lie sidewise. It's time to attempt the landing.

When you're fishing upstream, it's not hard to keep the fish ahead of you. Your pressure should be directed toward encouraging upstream runs, for if the fish gets below you, the downstream pull often adds just enough pressure to dislodge the hook. If the fish starts downstream, try to position yourself in front of him, and move toward him. Your blocking action will usually cause reversal to an upstream run.

Use the downstream flow to drift the fish toward your net, but guard against horsing him at it. The net should be submerged, its webbing floating freely behind. Sometimes, on seeing the net, the fish will get a surprisingly quick second wind and take off again. Be prepared to yield line, then repeat the wearing-down process. Don't chase your fish with the net, batting at him as if the net were a tennis racquet. Simply crouch low, while raising your rod hand (in which you are gripping retrieved slack) behind you until the fish drifts headfirst into the webbing—always headfirst.

When you are streamer fishing, strikes will be against the current. In order to eliminate its pressure against the fish, move below him. This should be done as you feel him out. While making your downstream move, care must be taken that line is kept taut, but pressure should be kept at a bare minimum while the fish is positioned against the current. When you get below him, more pressure may be applied.

In sizing up trout, a generally safe rule of thumb for determining when and when not to play is as follows: 10 inches and under will usually retrieve without your having to give line. Trout over 10 inches should be permitted to run. When extra-light leader tippets are used, however, care must be taken even with 10-inch trout.

The quick and powerful lunges of which heavier trout (14 inches and over) are capable render them better played from the reel. Line released and retrieved directly from and to the reel is line faster controlled than that held in slack coils. The beginning fly-rod angler, though, can develop a feel for the proper amount of pressure more quickly when handling line rather than when reeling it.

Enjoining a beginning angler to feel out his trout is about as helpful as telling a proven psychotic "to get hold of himself." For anxiety about losing those first fly-hooked trout is bound to lead to some exaggerated "guiding"; maybe even some horsing. Trout will be lost, but if the tyro persists in equating himself with a cautious boxer, the feeling-out and sizing-up process will become automatic.

I've seen this happen many times. So don't get discouraged if your initial playings and landings are on the sloppy side. With practice, losses will decline rapidly.

# CHAPTER 4

# *Streamers*

$A$s a fledgling angler, I was completely convinced that there were two important rules to follow in order to take more and bigger trout. The first: fish the deepest holes; the second: use minnows.

Twenty years of experience fishing in all parts of the continent have proved the first rule only partly right. As to the second, I'm convinced that I was correct enough, so long as "minnow imitations" can be substituted for minnows.

As we've discovered, freshly stocked trout seek the deeper holes until acclimated; then they move into riffles to forage. During most of the season then, it pays to fish the whole stream, not just deep pools. This is hard to do with live minnows. They'll easily drown in fast water, and various kinds of fastening devices notwithstanding, they often tear and lose shape and become ineffective or come off the hook. By way of preventing this, it's necessary to curtail casting.

Streamers preclude these difficulties. They're so easy to fish that some call them beginners' lures. Manipulation against a downstream flow eliminates problems of drag inherent in upstream presentation. When a dry fly is drifting back to you, for example, a deviation in the current can belly the line behind or in front of the fly and cause it to drag unnaturally. But when you're fishing against the current to begin with, it's only necessary to impart a minnowlike jerking action which activates hair or feathers and tantalizes trout. Also, the pull of the current simplifies the pickup for the back cast, not to mention that downstream handling reduces casting, a big help on small streams with lots of tree cover. Your streamer can simply be fed out with the current—as far as you care to drift it—before retrieving.

STREAMER PRESENTATION

Quartering streamers is very effective because it ensures covering the maximum amount of water in minimum time, enabling the fly to be presented to the greatest possible number of fish. When wading larger streams, simply cast at a 45-degree angle downstream toward the shoreline and allow the streamer to drift the desired distance. Then sweep it into midstream, retrieving in short jerks. Nine times out of ten this is the streamer's moment of truth—when it ends its free drift and swings into those first darting stabs against the current. After a step or two downstream, cast to the opposite bank. The same procedure should be followed as you fish toward one bank then the other as you walk your way downstream (Fig. 8).

When the streamer is drifting, it simulates a minnow or fingerling fish gliding lazily with the current; the jerking retrieve gives it the appearance of its natural counterpart working against the current.

In small streams, where wading isn't necessary, simply drift the streamer along the closest bank and quarter into the middle. Then cast to the far bank, and after drifting, quarter to

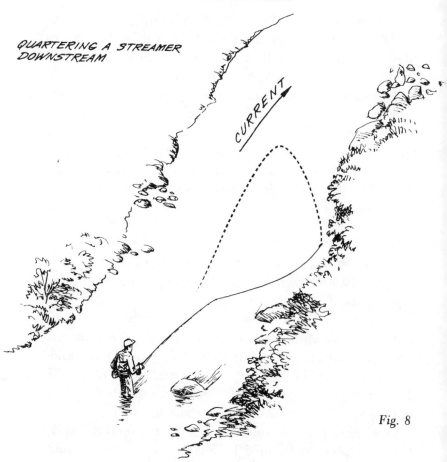

QUARTERING A STREAMER
DOWNSTREAM

CURRENT

Fig. 8

the middle, and so on. Whether on small streams or large, be sure to impart jerking motion when the streamer approaches the most likely looking spots. Recognizing them is known as water reading.

Your effectiveness as a streamer angler increases in direct proportion to your ability to read water. This is true, of course, in all fishing, but generally water reading provides more of an assist in fishing streamers than with wet flies or dries. A bulge in a smooth stretch or a rhythmic flashing in shallows signals a nymphing trout, and those calendar-art rises suggest surface feeding. In both instances you can mark your trout and fish to him with sunken or surface flies, respectively. Streamers, though, are mostly used to fish blind, and are sometimes referred to as fish finders. Usually considered high-water lures, streamers are most often fished in early season before fly life is active enough to bring feeding trout into view. In high, cloudy water, they're easier for trout to spot than smaller flies. Fast water activates them better than slow, and helps disguise their phoniness, an impossibility when they're fished in clear limpid water of late season. But streamers are not effective in any kind of rough water. They show to best advantage around deflectors, where trout don't have to fight the full force of the current. Hence, our pocket-hopping technique in Chapter 2. But there are deflecting phenomena other than those very obvious rock-hemmed pockets, and a good water reader will detect them.

One such—from whom I learned a lot about water reading twenty years ago—was an elderly minister. I can close my eyes and see him knee-deep in the lovely Tobyhanna in Pennsylvania's Pocono Mountains. As I describe his technique, see if you can count the various stream situations which he turned to his advantage.

Standing in the middle of a sharply riffled stretch the Reverend would false cast until a comfortable amount of line was in the air—about 30 feet. His brilliantly hued Supervisor streamer angled downstream toward the left shore, sinking and washing along a tempting-looking deep cut along the bank. When the line was all paid out, he guided the streamer into a wide quartering sweep, toward a riffled glide in midstream. Here he imparted a series of short, sharp jerks to the lure. The glide was worked three times: in its upper reaches, its middle, and at the tail.

From where I stood, smoking by a rhododendron bush, the streamer appeared to dart and zigzag like a frightened little minnow escaping the shadows of a log, where a hungry cannibal trout could well have been waiting. The Reverend then shot his streamer to the right bank, next moving a few steps downstream and casting to the left and then to the right before moving on. I am still awed at the effortless practicality of the Reverend's techniques. He leisurely covered the entire stream at a steady pace, wading as he cast, loitering here and there. No more time was spent on a fishy-looking bankside pool than on an innocuous-looking rock-lined pocket. In both, riffles in the forefront were used to drift the streamer at a right or left angle into the downstream extremity. Then he retrieved though the center.

He carefully guided his streamer into a quiet eddying flat formed by a gravel bar, again making use of rough headwaters to disguise the streamer's entrance. Then the quartering turn was effected.

Now the minister neared a current-breaking half-submerged boulder at stream center. He studied it for a second or two and cast slightly to the left, just off the edge of that smooth sheltered slick, hard against the boulder. I tensed as a large dark-amber dorsal fin broke water near the lure, but the fish refused. The Reverend tried him once more before shooting a cast to the edges of white water at the base of small waterfalls.

Let's run down the hot spots on which the Reverend concentrated: spots common to every mountain stream you'll fish (Fig. 9, Nos. 1-8).

First, there was that deep bankside cut (No. 1). The over-

FISHING THE STREAMER
DOWNSTREAM

Fig. 9

LEGEND

① DEEP BANKSIDE CUT
② LONG RIFFLED GLIDE
③ HALF-SUBMERGED LOG
④ DEEP SMOOTH POOL
⑤ POCKET WATER
⑥ FLAT
⑦ BOULDER
⑧ WATERFALL HOLE

⟶ CAST

⤵ PATH OF FLY IN WATER

🐟 TROUT

hung bank offered a shady hiding place. It was also a perfect feeding station where terrestrial insects could fall from shoreline grass and bushes. It's often worthwhile to make a retrieve or two flush against such bankside cuts before quartering to midstream.

Next the long riffled glide (No. 2). Note that the minister executed three quarterings. Since trout often lie in tiers, he worked the upper portion, the middle, and the lower.

Then there was the log (No. 3). Here was an ideal current-breaker, against which a trout could loaf in shadowed seclusion, ready to pounce on the Reverend's counterfeit minnow. Remember, teasing action was imparted as close to the upstream side of the log as possible.

Deep smooth pools (No. 4) must be handled with care. The minister knew that a cast to the middle of a quiet pool is almost sure to put down fish. So he dropped his streamer in the rougher water entering the pool, guiding its drift-in on either the right or left side so as to keep line out of the strike zone. When the streamer reached the pool's downstream extremity, it was quartered up through the center. The streamer's entrance did not frighten fish at pool center. And it had ample time to sink within range of bottom-hugging trout. Note that he handled pocket water (No. 5) in the same fashion. But as we learned in Chapter 2, pockets are usually more turbulent, hence easier to handle.

In flats (No. 6) rough water to the fore was also used to facilitate the streamer's entrance and disguise its phoniness.

The midstream boulder (No. 7), unlike the more impermanent log, had withstood wind, flood, and ice for years. Grinding action of ice against the upstream face of the boulder probably shoveled out a nice little holding pool at its bottom. No wonder a nice fish was raised here.

Holes at the bases of waterfalls are easy (No. 8) and the

heavy white water was used to hide the streamer's entry into the hole. But the line was kept to the sides of the falls. Had it been allowed to drift in the center, turbulence could have thrust it smack in the face of his quarry.

Bankside cuts, riffled glides, logs, deep pools, pockets, flats, boulders, and waterfalls—in that order—were phenomena noted and worked by the Reverend. Seek them out yourself, and when fishing them, don't forget to think like a trout before you make your cast. As you begin to sense when a streamer looks minnowlike to a trout and when it doesn't, you will become, like the minister, a water reader by instinct.

STREAMER SELECTION

In order properly to match streamers to different species of trout in their respective environments, we must be aware of their evolution.

As a pastime, fly fishing began about five hundred years ago in the lovely chalk-stream region of England. Early practitioners impaled live flies on hooks; given their relatively large hooks and the small size of the insects, this was difficult. So artificial fly imitations were born, not meant to be works of art but tied to look as buggy as their natural counterparts. Since baiting with minnows was easier, there was no need for imitations here, and had artificials been used they would have proved impractical, for the man-shy brown trout of those civilized waters would not have been easily fooled. In slow placid limestone (chalk) streams, any kind of artificial minnow (unlike smaller counterfeit flies) would have looked like just that, something artificial.

But the riffled and tumbling freestone mountain streams of North America disguised the phoniness of the earlier streamers by robbing trout of a close look. Also, rough water lent realistic movement to those first large feathered lures. While versions of their origin differ, it is established that streamers were used by the late Theodore Gordon around the turn of the century.

Tied on large long-shank hooks (Nos. 2 and 4), early streamers were objects of real beauty. Indeed, early tyers vied with one another for brilliance and distinctiveness in the manner of neighbors competing for top honors in Yuletide decorations. Thus many feathered concoctions were dubbed "Christmas trees." But they took fish.

The wary German (and English) brown trout had only been introduced to North America twenty-odd years before. Native American trout—the eastern brook and the western rainbow—were in heavy preponderance throughout largely unspoiled mountainous reaches of the continent. Unacquainted with the wiles of intruding fishermen and excited by those colorful lures, native trout struck with wild abandon. They were especially attracted by the pulsating flank feathers (Fig. 10). When pulled against the current, the feathers flattened; while drifting back, they billowed out from the hook's shank. Thus a series of upstream jerks, punctuated with short

Fig. 10

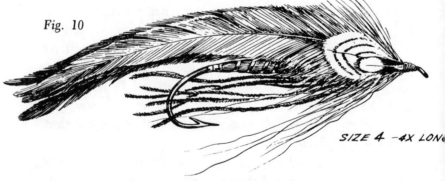

SIZE 4 -4X LON(

GRAY GHOST STREAMER

(ACTUAL SIZE)

drifts, resulted in what came to be known as breathing.

Notwithstanding the deadly attractiveness of the lures, rough water sometimes fouled the supple flank feathers on the hook. Stiffer material, such as deer- or squirrel-tail hair, proved to be the answer. Hence, the birth of the bucktail, or, as some called it, the bucktail streamer (Fig. 11).

*Fig. 11*

BUCKTAIL STREAMER
SIZE 8 - 3X LONG

Technically, feathered models were, and are, considered streamers and hair patterns called bucktails. But over the years both hair and feathered imitations of minnows and small fish have become known, generically, as streamers.

Whether tied with hair or feathers, America's initial contribution to fly angling worked, but it should be remembered, as attractors for unsophisticated wilderness trout. Early streamers were brightly dressed because they were frequently off-shoots of wet-fly patterns of the period. Most wet flies were colorful in the extreme and bore little resemblance to natural fly life, and since native trout were patsies for them it was logical that streamers should approximate their progenitors.

But the onrush of civilization heralded the decline of native trout. While the eastern brookie languished in the face of stepped-up fishing pressure and warmer waters, resulting from deforestation, the brown was more successful in resisting both. Consequently, he took over from the brook. He was not nearly so partial to bright attractor lures and he had to be deceived with more lifelike imitations.

So with the development of the dry fly—which the free-rising brown took with alacrity—American fly angling assumed the character of England's; imitations of insects became more pronounced. A side effect was the development of streamer patterns imitative of the trout's food fish. True, there had been some such patterns earlier; the Gray Ghost was supposed to ape the New England smelt, and there were artificials, too, of the little stickleback, the yellow shiner, and others. Most, though, bore but scant resemblance to their natural prototypes.

Streamers got their first real boost as deceiver lures with the development of the Black-Nose Dace bucktail by Art Flick and the late Preston Jennings in the 1930's. It imitated the one bait fish known to all who fish for trout anywhere in the continent: the minnow with the distinctive lateral black streak. Immediately it became known as a terrific trout-taker.

A streamer, of course, can't come close to being a dead ringer for a fish. Deceiver streamer patterns are meant to be impressionistic, to record the vividness and force of the first impression without elaborate detail. This is exactly the effect

UNDERWATER IMPRESSIONS OF BLACK-NOSE DACE MINNOW

that, say, a Black-Nose Dace imitation should have on a trout. In swift riffled water, he catches only a fleeting glimpse of a darting dace—or its counterfeit. Deceiver theory holds that when he gets a hazy impression of a brownish back, that dark lateral streak above a shiny belly, chances of conning a strike from him are excellent (Fig. 12).

Another effective deceiver pattern, developed by Ray Bergman in the thirties, is the Brown Squirrel Tail. The red tag (at the tail) against a dark back and a yellow, gold-ribbed body contributes to the mating-season appearance of darker-colored male minnows.

The famous Muddler Minnow, tied by Don Gapin, is a deadly imitation of the little sculpin, common throughout the country.

My own Little Brown Trout was designed to accommodate the cannibalistic impulse of brownies toward their young.

Cynics may scoff at the idea of imitating little fish with hair and feathers, but there is one nontheoretical conclusion which can be taken as gospel about deceiver patterns; they are more like actual small fish when a generally dull coloration is used. No one ever saw a minnow colored up like a Royal Coachman streamer. Except for their silvery bellies (sometimes flanks as well), young fish and minnows rarely sport bright

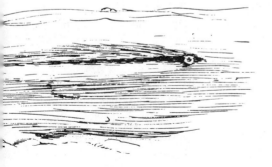

Fig. 12

ND BUCKTAIL STREAMER

hues. As nonminnows mature, they do, but not when they're in and just emerging from the fingerling stage. I'm convinced that this accounts for my greater success with deceivers, as against attractor streamers, over many years; particularly when fishing over well-educated trout of hard-fish waters. And always over the more wary brownies.

But colorful attractors have their place. On early spring's high roily water, the loudest streamer in your fly book can be better seen from greater distance by more fish. Lean and hungry after their long winter dormancy, holdover trout are ready for any kind of mouthful. As noted in Chapter 2, their freshly stocked cousins also fall hard for colorful patterns. So do wilderness brookies of the far North (known in Maine and Canada as squaretails), arctic charr, and landlocked salmon. Sometimes these fish are so unfamiliar with lures of any kind that they've been known to strike cigarette butts.

Four famous attractor streamers with which I've done very well are the Royal Coachman, the Parmachene Belle, the Supervisor, and the Light Edson Tiger bucktail.

When fishing is slow, attractor streamers can be of benefit as fish finders. A particularly bright one sometimes annoys a somnolent trout enough to evoke a swirling pass. Not necessarily a strike; the streamer is not realistic enough. But at least the fish will have revealed his whereabouts. Then the angler can switch to a duller deceiver pattern and very often take him.

The success of this approach has led me to coin the term "attractor-deceiver" for patterns with enough attracting qualities to interest fish and with coloration sufficiently realistic to dupe them at the same time. The Montreal streamer has a sparkling silver tinsel body for attraction, while its drab maroons tend to give the appearance of a dusky-colored minnow.

The Silver Darter streamer is bright enough to be seen from a great distance, and it has the familiar black streak of a dace. It also takes on the white gossamer glimmer of the common shiner. The Gray Ghost was meant to simulate the fresh-water smelt of New England, where it can be used as a deceiver. But elsewhere, its bright gold tinsel-ribbed body qualifies it as an attractor. The Mickey Finn is well known as an attractor for brook trout. But in trout streams fed by, or emptying into, warmer lakes, it can work as a deceiver. For it has the orange-red hues of young sunfish, which often work their way from lake to stream and are eaten by larger trout.

We've discussed twelve streamer patterns; four deceivers, four attractors, and four attractor-deceivers. There are many more in each category; indeed, any streamer can be placed in one. The recommended reading list in Chapter 12 provides additional patterns with which you can familiarize yourself. Over the years you can engage in the fascinating experimentation involved in matching patterns and conditions, and thus broaden your own list.

But for now these twelve patterns are all that you will need. I know some experienced anglers who stick to this basic list (or variations of it, which adhere to attractor-deceiver theory) whenever and wherever they fish streamers. For handy reference, here is the list, by category:

### Deceivers

Black-Nose Dace, Brown Squirrel Tail, Muddler Minnow, Little Brown Trout

### Attractors

Royal Coachman, Parmachene Belle, Supervisor, Light Edson Tiger

### Attractor-Deceivers

Montreal, Silver Darter, Gray Ghost, Mickey Finn

Unlike those large-size 2 and 4 early streamers, the preponderance today (for trout) runs in sizes 4, 6, and 8, on long-shank hooks. Most anglers feel that these sizes more closely approximate the size of trout's food fish. Also, they're large enough to be spotted in high water. There are many smaller fry fish, but since these are harder to single out in high water, there's no sense in imitating them. All of which have contributed to the popularization of the above streamer sizes, as well as to the belief that streamers are high-water lures.

But why should trout be less cannibalistic in low water; especially in late summer when aquatic fly hatches taper off and they must scrounge for not always plentiful food? Food fish are now in demand. And in late summer's shallow water, trout can more readily spot tiny fish. But standard-size streamers are usually too large for shrunken streams. Not only do they tend to frighten and put down trout, but even when successfully presented, in low clear water, their phoniness simply can't be disguised.

To lick this problem veteran fly-angler John S. Wise, Jr., developed streamerettes—small streamers tied on size 10 and 12 long-shank hooks (Fig. 13). As a result of his permitting

*Fig. 13*

STREAMERETTE  -  SIZE 10
(ACTUAL SIZE)

me to write about them in *Sports Afield,* they are now available in both attractor and deceiver patterns at many sporting
goods stores and most catalog houses, so streamer fishing
need no longer be confined to high-water conditions. Streamerettes should be fished exactly like their larger counterparts.
They are also double-barrel lures. Duller deceivers (especially
the Muddler Minnow) are deadly, fished upstream as large
nymphs.

To sum up on streamers: Study the situations in Figure 9.
While fishing, look for them. Work them like the minister.
Remember to keep moving. Don't allow fetching-looking
pools to hold you up more than a few minutes. Cover as much
water as possible, and as you do, keep trying to read it. As
water reading becomes involuntary, you can be confident that
the remainder of your introduction to fly fishing is a downhill
course.

# CHAPTER 5

# The Wet Fly–Nymph

It's a safe bet that year in and year out sunken flies take more trout than streamers and dry flies combined. In this chapter we will discuss how to make wet flies even more productive by combining their most potent characteristics with those of nymphs in what we will call the wet fly–nymph technique.

Sunken flies were the ancestors of the other categories of artificial flies. The first was tied in Macedonia around A.D. 200, but dry flies did not evolve until late in the nineteenth century. Streamers and nymphs followed in relatively quick succession.

The weight of large, crudely made iron and bronze hooks was probably responsible for the wet fly's protracted period of dominance. Floatability could only be achieved by refined metallurgical processes occasioned by the Industrial Revolution, but early exponents of the wet fly got on very well without its later derivatives. And well they should have. The life span of the trout's favorite fare, aquatic flies, is spent almost entirely as larvae on the stream bed—where, at times, they are available food—and as nymphs, on which trout can feed effortlessly during their slow, surfaceward ascent to turn into winged flies. Then there are mature flies (terrestrial as well as aquatic) sunken by rough water. At all times—except during the height of a fly hatch—subsurface are more prevalent than surface flies. Small wonder that sunken imitations of fly life are still the deadliest trout lures of all.

Generally, wet flies and nymphs are treated as separate stages of fly life requiring differing methods of presentation. Wet flies are usually quartered downstream, like streamers. Perhaps this classical method is a throwback to the days of heavy 12-foot rods and horsehair lines—unwieldy instruments for accurate upstream casts and brisk timely pickups necessitated by swift and erratic currents. It was more leisurely to cast cross-stream at a 45-degree angle and permit a long drift followed by a sweeping upstream retrieve.

Read almost any tract on the wet fly and this will still be the recommended technique, for good reason, as it still gets results. The proposition is that the fly's drift simulates a sinking natural and provides it an opportunity to get below the surface. Then, when quartered, it will rise like a natural fly moving up to hatch. The theory is supposed to be borne out by the fact that most strikes occur during the quartering action, but what trout ever saw a hatching fly proceeding as if jet-propelled into a roundhouse sweep against the current? To the contrary, it must ride with it. Only a few of the larger species of flies can make headway against the flow, and a very weak flow it must be.

I certainly don't want to cause doubt as to the success of classic wet-fly presentation, for it has the blessing of expert anglers from time out of memory, but I do submit that it is unnatural. And to those who protest that it works, I would suggest that they improve on it by substituting streamers for wet flies. After all, against-the-current propulsion simulates minnow action, not that of flies. So a more fishy counterfeit would seem to be in order.

The traditional nymph method calls for an upstream delivery followed by a downstream drift, and this is thoroughly realistic. The imitation drifts or bounces along the bottom, rising and falling, at the mercy of the current, just like the real article. And this is why chips should be put on the nymph angler as against the practitioner of classic wet-fly angling, any time, anywhere.

Why have we dwelt on a seemingly hairsplitting discussion about what should constitute proper wet-fly technique and what should not—especially when the classic approach takes fish? Simply to enable you to become more proficient faster with wet flies, and, over the long pull, to increase your take of trout.

As noted, artificial nymphs imitate unhatched flies in their creeper or crawler stage, and wet flies can imitate the nymph in the act of hatching. Now you can't present an artificial nymph so that it will appear to creep along the bottom. But you can let it drift along with the current near the bottom, thus simulating a nymph getting ready to hatch. At this stage many begin struggling to emerge from their protective shuck. There's no better representation of this metamorphosis than the wet fly, its flaccid hackle fibers trembling in the current like protruding legs, its glistening wet, flat-back wings resembling natural counterparts in the act of breaching their transparent coating (Fig. 14).

Again, the charge of hairsplitting may be leveled. For exquisitely tied nymph imitations do take trout, but it's really the traditionalists who are the hairsplitters. In fast-flowing streams trout have scant opportunity to scrutinize nymphs. So the exactness of an imitation as to the number of antennae,

Fig. 14

UNDERWATER IMPRESSIONS OF NATURAL NYMPH (LEFT)
AND WET FLY (RIGHT).

tail fibers, and body segments becomes academic enough to
be laughable. Plainly, trout don't give a damn. If they did,
plastic nymphs, molded from natural ones, would score far
and away more effectively than hand-tied offerings. The fact
is, they don't.

Trout see their watery world as a food-carrying conveyor
belt, but it does not often run smoothly. As they face the flow
awaiting food, the fish anticipate the erratic ride that a
deflector-ridden current imparts. They must concentrate on
their food's movement more than its anatomy, and even at its
clearest, the moving envelope of water blends back and forth
from translucency to transparency, as dancing riffles meld
with placid flats, tumbling rapids with quiet pools. Stated
briefly, trout are only permitted—as in the case of streamers
—an impressionistic view of a hatching or sunken fly. So they
must be served something suggesting same. In moving water a
wet fly fits the bill better than a nymph imitation.

I learned the effectiveness of wet flies fished nymph-fashion
twenty years ago during Opening Day on a stream in Pennsylvania's Pocono Mountains. This experience cannot be
ascribed to beginner's luck. For its results have been tested

every year since, on Opening Day, on the same water.

The stream contained then, as it does now, a heavy pre-ponderance of cagey, naturally bred brown trout over the stocked variety. Water temperatures as low as 40 degrees in mid-April always make fish sluggish in the extreme; even large streamers rarely move them. Deep-fished nymphs work better. During early hours on my first outing, a store-bought dead-ringer Hendrickson nymph yielded several bumps and two fish. Then I happened on an elderly regular of the stream who advised that wet flies, not nymphs, were the answer. I protested that wet-fly fishermen had been doing nothing, to which he answered that they "weren't fishing them right." He produced a Leadwing Coachman wet fly, rubbed it in wet gravel, and offered it, suggesting that I fish it like a nymph. I did, and it was murder. Traditionalist wet-fly anglers, pa-tiently quartering with the time-honored hand-twist retrieve against the current, took few fish because their flies passed too high over the low-lying trout. Streamer fishermen did better because, while their lures were often high, they were big enough for trout to see better, hence they had some attracting qualities. Were brook trout prevalent, streamers probably would have created mayhem, but those sophisticated stream-bred browns are always tougher to take on streamers. Natu-rally, nymphs fished deep scored well. But the few of us work-ing dull-colored wet flies like nymphs were the most successful. Our hatching-nymph imitations were temptingly realistic.

More exacting imitations of nymphs are useful in placid streams and still pools. Here trout get a better view of insect anatomy. That's why a nymph, instead of a wet fly, was rec-ommended for deep fishing of the trout pond in Chapter 2.

That old gentleman messed up the fly to make a point. It must look "bedraggled," he said, adding that it should appear to trout as "buggy looking as a swatted fly on a fresh tablecloth appears to us." Over the years the simile stuck. I still find myself, ritualistically perhaps, rubbing a Leadwing in the stream's gravel before that first cast of the season.

It should be pointed out here that competitive anglers are bores to be avoided at all costs. We will touch on this when discussing stream etiquette later on; I only mention comparative scores here to demonstrate the efficacy of the wet fly–nymph.

WET FLY–NYMPH PRESENTATION

Presentation of the wet fly–nymph calls for the classic sink-and-draw method of nymph angling (Fig. 15). The fly should

FISHING THE NYMPH UPSTREAM:
CAST UPSTREAM, NYMPH DROPS INTO BROKEN WATER (A).
NYMPH PERMITTED TO SINK CLOSE TO BOTTOM (B).
SPEEDING UP RETRIEVE CAUSES NYMPH TO RISE (C).

Fig. 15

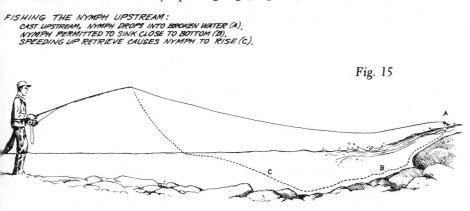

be cast ahead of you upstream; and before it completes its drift back to you, raise your rod tip slowly while gathering slack in your line hand. This will cause your fly to ascend like an insect about to hatch. Some fishermen object that upstream delivery of the wet fly necessitates its sinking before it rises— not the case when it's quartered downstream. There is nothing unreal about a sinking wet fly. Many natural nymphs begin their rise and sink again—sometimes repeatedly—before hatching successfully. Also, in shallow flats and glides, your fly does not have far to sink, and, as noted, riffles and rough water entering pools, glides, and flats, hide the fly's sinking action.

The drift-back method—as opposed to against-current retrieving—results in slack-line fishing, so trout can't as readily hook themselves as they often do on a more taut line. You can reduce the problem by taking in line fast enough to keep floating slack at a minimum. In other words, try to keep a straight line drifting back to you, not loops and coils. A short but sharp upward jerk of the rod will often insure positive hooking.

You will experience false alarms. A deep-drifting fly will sometimes snare on submerged obstructions. You will strike, snag, and occasionally lose a fly, so always have a few duplicates of flies you intend to fish. You won't be overloaded. For you will find—as with streamers—that wet fly–nymph fishing calls for few patterns.

Early season's high water will often make it difficult to get your fly deep enough. A custom fly tyer can supply your favorite early season patterns dressed on weighted hooks. If you can't locate a nearby tyer, write to one of the supply houses dealing in fly-fishing supplies. Weighted wet flies (and nymphs) will usually sink deep enough, but they increase the possibilities of snagging. So be sure to have plenty of extras.

On your 7½-foot fly rod a size 10 or 12 weighted fly will not feel too unwieldy, but the increased weight may contribute to inaccurate casts. Sinking lines, while they do cause some underwater snagging, are often easier to handle. Lines are available for fishing just below the surface, at middle depths, and deep down. Your rod and most medium-sized trout streams (approximately 20 feet across) call for slow-sinking line during high-water conditions. On larger streams, with a lot of heavy water, a fast-sinking line is more efficient (See Chapter 7). Throughout most of the season, though, floating line is

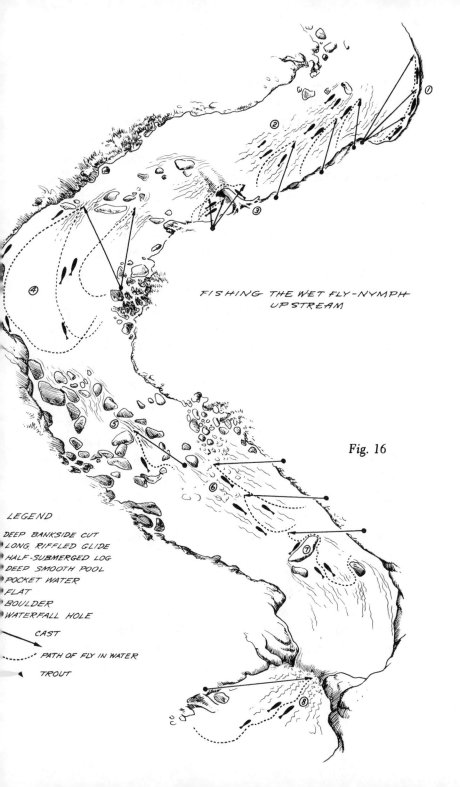

FISHING THE WET FLY-NYMPH
UPSTREAM

Fig. 16

LEGEND

① DEEP BANKSIDE CUT
② LONG, RIFFLED GLIDE
③ HALF-SUBMERGED LOG
④ DEEP SMOOTH POOL
⑤ POCKET WATER
⑥ FLAT
⑦ BOULDER
⑧ WATERFALL HOLE

→ CAST

---- PATH OF FLY IN WATER

◄ TROUT

usually satisfactory. Depths are rarely so great as to preclude adequate sinking, and ease of handling compensates for those few times when they are.

Light hooking with wet fly–nymphs will be responsible for many a lost trout. But when trout are fooled (as their slow take proves) by a good imitation of food, more fish will sample your fly than is the case when they're merely attracted. So misses notwithstanding, in the long run you will net more.

Let's take the same stream diagram used for streamers (Fig. 16). But you will now be nymphing upstream.

Observe Number 1, the bankside cut. These are usually narrow, so trout must lie in tandem. The closest group to you is fished first, then the middle group, and finally the top, your technique being exactly the same as that used next, in the long riffled glide, Number 2. Observe that here trout lie roughly in tiers. At risk of oversimplification we have positioned them in three lines: the first at the lower lip of the riffle, closest to you; the next in the middle of the stretch; the last at the top.

If you cast to the top, a settling line will put down the middle and bottom tier. Your first casts should be made to the lip, with only the leader being permitted in the strike zone. Since your fly should light within a dozen feet of the riffled end, it will have little opportunity to sink but don't worry about this. The lip is usually shallow, so the fly has little distance to sink and fish don't have to rise to any appreciable degree.

Should you snag a first-tier fish, chances are that his mates will scurry to the fore. Sometimes they will put down some in the next tier as well. This is particularly true of the scary brown trout—less so the brook. But in larger, well-riffled stretches (which help disguise your leader), spooking is of little moment so long as you keep the line out of sight of the tier over which you're working.

The second tier will often be in the deepest part of the glide. Your next series of casts, then, should be well to the head, so that the fly will have time to settle before reaching the trout's deep lie. The binocular vision of the trout extends about 20 to 30 feet ahead within a narrow field of view. He is blind from the top of his head rearward. If you are quiet in your approach, he won't notice you, but you must keep that line out of his straightaway line of sight. The first tier presents no problem because your line is out of the area being fished. If you cast directly up the glide over the second tier, however, you will run a good chance of dropping line in full view of the fish. That being true, it's best if you position yourself either to the right or left of the glide and deliver your fly from a slight angle. A sidearm, or horizontal, cast sometimes is helpful in such situations.

The top tier is easy. Again, keeping your line free of the center, cast well to the fore of the riffled entrance and let your fly wash in. As at the lip, it won't have to sink far as entrance water is usually shallow.

Riffled glides provide excellent water for the wet fly–nymph. Not only does the broken water hide the leader, it deaccentuates your shadow and movement and gives the fly a bumpy realistic ride, a brisk enough one to rob trout of too close a look at it.

Now we face the log again—its downstream side (Number 3). A flat is created in which the flow is reduced sufficiently to permit a lie for a trout or two. They're not likely to be smack against the log's bottom laterally, as on the upstream side, where it serves as much as a shield as a current breaker. Rather, they will often be backed off, facing it. But not so far back as to get into the resumed current. This positioning gives them a good shot at food drifting under or washing over the log. So don't zero in on the log. Place the first cast just to the fore of the area where the current strengthens again. Then work succeeding casts up to the log. A cast over the log is often in order, but try to get only the leader over the log; permit a short drift. Be sure to lift your fly into the back cast before it's swept against the log and fouled. Sometimes that trout lying lengthwise against the log on the upstream side will move out and seize your fly just before you're forced to lift it.

Remember to keep line from the center of deep still pools. Your best approach for Number 4 is to work from an angle and cast to the broken backwaters feeding the pool. Allow your fly to wash down into its center. Since it's very easy to telegraph your presence near still pools, it's often wise to cast from a kneeling position, taking advantage of any cover you can find.

For Number 5 turn back to Chapter 2 and review the upstream handling of those rock-hemmed pockets. As was noted, these are easy to fish because their surface is generally more agitated than that of pools. But when fishing larger pockets, it's wise to work them like the pools. Thus you will be guarding against getting line in the strike zone.

Large flats (Number 6) are fished in the same marching-cast manner used along cuts and in riffled glides. Your first cast should be to the lip with only the leader in the riffle. As in pools, succeeding casts are angled from the sides. Often the riffled backwater can be used, as in pools, to carry the fly to the flat's center.

Note the downstream flat created by the boulder (Number 7). Handle this flat as you did the log's. A quick pickup on the upstream side is sometimes necessary if the boulder is moss-covered. If not, allow the fly to wash against the boulder where water purls on its upstream side. Guide it around into the slick immediately behind and permit it to drift into the flat. Sometimes your previous casts to the flat won't raise fish, but the drift around the boulder will. Possibly the realistic bouncing action, imparted to the fly by broken current as it enters the downstream slick, is responsible.

Finally, those holes at the bases of waterfalls (Number 8). Cast your fly to the white water at the base. But, remember, you're not fishing the white water; it's to be used to get the fly deep in the hole. So allow plenty of time for the fly to get swamped and thrashed around, like a swamped insect. Once it is well sunk, drag it very slowly along the bottom and up, like a nymph beginning its ascent.

FLY SELECTION

Since your presentation is meant to deceive, logic dictates that the fly should deceive as well. We've noted that the Leadwing Coachman wet fly is dull colored and buggy looking, particularly so when its green-black peacock body is wet. Another plus is the fact that it imitates the *Isonychia Bicolor,* a May fly that, unlike most, hatches throughout spring and summer. So a good supply in your fly box is a must, in sizes 10 and 12.

The Hendrickson and Quill Gordon are very common early season May flies. The Hendrickson wet is best imitated in sizes 10 and 12, the Quill Gordon wet in 12 or 14. Since both of these flies have a bluish-gray cast, I often use a wet Iron Blue Dun 12 to imitate either, especially when there's doubt as to which is the most active at a given time.

From early to midseason, stone flies are often prevalent. An imitation of the large *Perla Capitata* is an excellent producer.

If you follow the practice of most fly anglers, your wet-fly fishing will taper off as the season progresses, and increased surface-fly activity calls for the use of dry flies. Still, there will be times when surface flies are not in evidence; and times when they are, but fish aren't interested.

In midspring, some important May-fly nymphs are in motion, hatching or about to hatch—the March Brown, the Green Drake, and the Ginger Quill. Since the Ginger Quill is often late in emerging, it's an ideal wet fly for late-season use. And its small size renders its use on low water more effective than larger patterns which are more apt to scare trout on delivery. The Light Cahill is also important in late season. Being small, too, it's an excellent pattern on which to concentrate. The one exception to this low-water-small-fly rule is the Leadwing Coachman, a continual trout-taker no matter what conditions prevail.

It's wise to carry a few nymph equivalents of each of the above-mentioned wet patterns. As noted, these will be helpful in still water.

So here's your line-up of wet flies:

| EARLY SEASON | | | MIDSEASON | | |
|---|---|---|---|---|---|
| | | Sizes | | | Sizes |
| Leadwing Coachman | | #10, #12 | Leadwing Coachman | | #10, #12 |
| Quill Gordon | | #12, #14 | Green Drake | | #10 |
| Hendrickson | | #10, #12 | March Brown | | #10 |
| Iron Blue Dun | #10, | #12, #14 | Ginger Quill | | #12, #14 |
| Stone Fly | | #10 | | | |

| LATE SEASON | |
|---|---|
| | Sizes |
| Leadwing Coachman | #12 |
| Ginger Quill | #12 |
| Light Cahill | #14 |

We've made no mention of some of the old favorite wet-fly attractor patterns because wet fly–nymph fishing is entirely based on deception. There is, however, one situation in which bright old standby wet flies (Royal Coachman, Parmachene Belle, Silver Doctor, etc.) are invaluable. When you're night fishing in areas of weak current, they are very effective as imitations of large nocturnal insects, swamped and struggling. Sizes 8 or 10, fished in tandem (one on a dropper, as in Fig. 17) with quartering, streamerlike action, are often deadly.

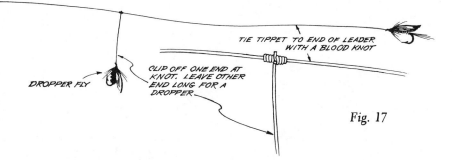

Fig. 17

Big trout that in daytime are less susceptible to attractor lures usually feed more carelessly at night. Darkness and a weak current render against-the-flow presentation more natural than would be the case in daylight.

Effective handling of the wet fly–nymph—like that of streamers—requires a conscious effort in seeking those various current-deflecting situations. Presentation will come easily with practice. Remember that many an excellent caster does not do as well as the mediocre one who, thinking like a trout, knows where they should be.

# CHAPTER 6

# The Dry Fly

The dry fly is widely considered the quintessential lure in all angling, so it's not surprising that many deem it the most difficult to fish. Actually, its handling need not be so exacting as that of the wet fly when fished upstream, and were these chapters arranged purely by degree of difficulty, we should have taken up the dry fly before the wet and nymph. But since the dry is derived from the wet—both naturally and artificially—proper sequence dictates that the sunken precede the surface fly. Not to mention that while water reading is basic to both, it is central to subsurface methods. Thus, its earlier introduction with wets makes dry-fly angling all the easier to master.

For example, unlike the case of nymphs and minnows, a trout's take of natural-floating flies is visible to the angler, so when trout are rising, there is no need for underwater prospecting. In the English chalk-stream fashion, you single out your trout and "fish to the rise." When they're not rising but the presence of surface flies indicates that they should be, your previously acquired knowledge of water reading will be crucial.

## DRY-FLY PRESENTATION

Basically, the nymph and dry-fly approaches are the same, so the wet fly–nymph diagram (Fig. 16) can be used with reference to dry-fly presentation. Since water is often lower during dry-fly season, however, some situations require variations in casting strategy. Our main purpose here is to enable you to capitalize on these sometimes difficult situations.

Even the most exact dry-fly imitations require moving and preferably some broken water for effective presentation—especially over wily brown trout. For an artificial fly is an inert form, and there's little you can do to provide lifelike action that water can't. Like the hatching nymph, the mature fly is at the mercy of the current, so your surface offering should behave like your subsurface one. It should drift with the flow; the more it bounces, the better, for trout will view its anatomy less clearly. Also, the bouncing action has its attracting side; when you fish dry, then, be sure to concentrate on riffled or broken stretches; not, however, so rough as to sink the fly. While rough water can be a boon in getting wet flies down, only heavily hackled dries with stiff fibers should be chanced in the heart of turbulent water.

Avoid also dead water, where movement is so slight that the water appears stagnant. In the spring, large flats (Fig. 16, 6) can be worked in their entirety, but in summer central portions can get so low as to render casting useless. Standing well back, work the entire length of the downstream lip—then the upstream riffles, disregarding the center.

My obsession is the converting of bait fishermen to flies. I revel in the ease with which they take to dry flies—after surmounting one hurdle inbred in all who begin by bait fishing for trout, which the following experience will, I hope, spare you.

One convert had done well with streamers and wet fly–nymphs before I introduced him to dries. Small yellow stone flies were moving that midsummer afternoon, so I suggested a Cream Variant, adding that he stick to riffled water. Then we split up. Fish were patsies for the fly. A couple of hours later I was resting at our appointed meeting place, but my partner failed to appear. I finally found him where I expected to, dejectedly casting into a large still pool. He bitterly griped about sweating out the Cream Variant and having nothing to show but one little brookie.

My partner's difficulty lay right at his feet. In that placid pool, trout couldn't help but sense his approach, and even if he were very careful about his movements, an almost invisible leader would have been mandatory. Ruefully, he admitted his error, adding that he "couldn't pass up such a nice spot." I ventured that when you see them they usually sense you and that it's best to move along.

He had unconsciously reverted to his worm-fishing days. Many early-season worm fishermen get so accustomed to seeking out big holes that they find it hard to kick the habit when going to flies. Like this fellow, they tend to waste a lot of time casting over spooked trout, but once I got my companion to move to the riffled stretches, he did beautifully and was so gratified that often he passes up the quiet pools altogether. Be sure to apply the above-mentioned rule of thumb for shallow flats and to the stream at large; concentrate your casts on riffled water. Placid stretches often become so shallow as to allow trout no sense of protection, thus they head for riffled tails and headwaters and pocket water, where surface turbulence is increased by encircling rocks. So instead of wading upstream, it's often advisable to hike the shoreline and hunt such water. You'll stand less chance of spooking fish, and you won't be as tempted to waste time on those pools and flats where fish are most difficult.

When fishing over brook trout, or any species that has been recently stocked, flushing can be an interesting and deadly method. Find a pool with sun-bathing trout and a well-riffled head, and wade into the tail, and flush the trout forward to the riffles. Remain stock-still for several minutes, then cast to the head. Its rough water will play that disguising role, so far as you and your leader are concerned. No longer spooked, brookies will often rise beautifully to your dancing fly. Stream-bred browns are usually too flighty for the flushing tactic.

Another effective low-water method is to fish the breeze. Again, pick a placid stretch, keep well hidden, and wait for a breeze to riffle its surface. Then cast. Trout will now see only the settling fly, not the leader. Whenever I'm fishing one of my favorite streams on a day with intermittent breezes, I make for a beaver dam which has backed up the flow into a large still pool. I relax on a boulder behind the dam until a slight gust breaks up the pool's sheen. Then, crouching behind the dam, I shoot a short cast just over it. I rarely fail to raise a fish. Even its play fails to undo my second presentation—farther in—maybe five minutes later. But each cast is made completely at the whim of the breeze.

Still another approach to low water is so obvious as to merit little discussion. Use the dim light of early morning or late evening to hide the leader, which can be as obvious as an anchor chain in broad daylight.

Above all, remember one basic rule about low water: make each pocket and riffled stretch a little fishing trip in itself. Avoid placid water like the plague unless you're blessed with fish rising in it and ruffling the water, flushable fish, breezes, or weak lighting. Remember, too, that streams are often virtually deserted in late summer, especially when water is low, so you should have a maximum amount of water with un-spooked trout to yourself. Keep these tips in mind, and you'll very likely take more than under "normal" conditions.

From mid- to late season, crystal-clear water requires a longer and finer leader. Nine feet tapered to 5X is usually adequate, and this can be bought as a standard pack, so you won't have to splice it yourself. Choice of leaders, their preparation, and tying will be discussed in Chapter 7. The level line which you began with will be satisfactory on smaller streams as long casts (over 30 feet) are rarely necessary. On larger streams, rivers, or lakes—where longer casts might be required —it's wise to invest in a weight forward or torpedo taper line. More about line, too, in Chapter 7.

With the dry fly, false casting becomes more than useful in measuring distance, as with the sunken fly. A snappy false cast between each real one serves to dry the fly. Dry-fly preparations are available as assists and they will be taken up in Chapter 7. Don't expect any dry-fly preparations to work without false casts, however; they won't. So permit the false casting of dry flies to become involuntary.

To a lesser degree than wets, dries are subject to drag (Fig. 18). Drag results from variations in the current in which the

*Fig. 18*

fly, leader, and line are floating. Thus the fly will ride either faster or slower than line and leader and will not duplicate the drift of natural flies. "Mending" line will correct this. Cast with a loop in your line so that slack permits the fly a free drift (Fig. 19).

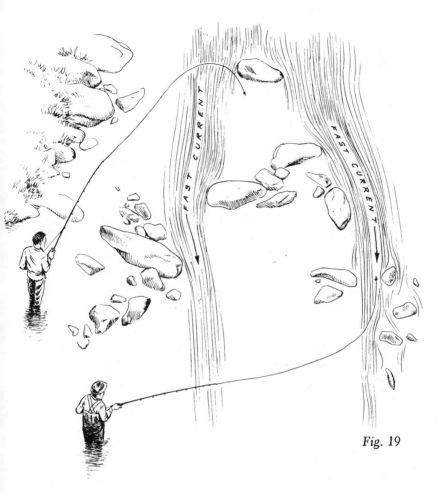

Fig. 19

LOOP OR CURVE CAST TO THE RIGHT (UPPER) PERMITS FLY TO FLOAT LONGER IN EDDY
BEFORE DRAG SETS IN. LOOP CAST TO THE LEFT (LOWER) RESULTS IN LONGER
DRAG-FREE FLOAT IN CURRENT.

FLY SELECTION

Since hatched flies are in full view of the angler, he is
tempted to imitate specific naturals with their artificial counterparts. This practice, known as "matching the hatch," is

considered important because trout often feed selectively on a single hatch of flies when more than one hatch is on the water. There is a common belief that one must be something of an entomologist to match hatches, but this is erroneous. Beginning fly anglers—as well as experienced ones whose knowledge of a stream's fly life is limited—can take trout on dry flies through seasonal hatch matching. By way of substantiating the merit of this novel approach I will touch briefly on my own introduction to it. Keep it in mind, for it may spare you an inferiority complex when you're regaled by experts on the esoteric art of hatch matching.

I don't remember what kinds of May flies were hatching that lovely evening almost twenty years ago on central Pennsylvania's Spring Creek, but there were several hatches of differing sizes. The fading twilight left little time for trial-and-error experimentation; downstream a fisherman's rod was set in a throbbing arch while a hefty brown-tail walked, plunged, and bolted clear before being led to net. Anxious to get the formula, I picked my way downstream as the angler creeled his catch and cast again. In a few minutes there was a frightful boil of white water. I was sure he was into a granddaddy. But then I detected a lateral motion in his rod and realized he was playing two fish at the same time.

In answer to my congratulations this Penn State professor laughed and said that he was "just lucky" and didn't like hooking two trout at the same time anyway, "like trying to keep two chess games going at the same time."

It turned out that because of weak eyesight the professor tied his leader with a dropper before going out. If a fly was lost, his spare meant he didn't need to tie on another. "But suppose you put on the wrong one?" I asked. "How can you know ahead of time what flies you'll have to match?"

He pointed to thick spectacles and noted that even with

them he couldn't tell one fly from another. He went on to explain that in early season a trout's favorite May flies are usually of average size and colored varying shades of gray. So from mid-April to mid-May he figured the odds heavily in favor of any kind of gray-blue or slate-colored dry fly, sizes 12 or 14. Even if corresponding naturals weren't on the water, he counted on the size and color's being familiar enough to raise fish.

It was all very interesting, but this theory seemed too simple. I was so little impressed that I never got the professor's name, or soon forgot it. I put him down as a nice fellow having a lucky evening. But accumulating years of dry-fly experience tended to verify his thinking—at least to my satisfaction. So did the opinion of some anglers, more experienced than myself, whose approach to dry flies was practical rather than esoteric. One such was my teacher from the very beginning, John Stauffer, a veteran of forty years.

Like the professor, John believed that gray flies are deadly early in the season, that in midseason the basic color of major hatches is brownish—generally somewhat larger than the earlier flies. For late season he recommended smaller patterns, mostly creams and whites. He added that these rules of thumb are effective anywhere east of the Rockies and most places west of them.

Since wet flies are not so regularly fished during mid- and late season, it was necessary to recommend only a few basic patterns. But if dries can be necessary in early season, they're indispensable later on. Thus there are potentially many more dry patterns than wet ones to pick from. So as to simplify choosing the right fly for the right conditions, I hit on the idea of developing several dry-fly patterns representative of size, color, and silhouette of the entire season's major May-fly hatches: the variant dry flies.

Differing concepts of variants have evolved with the years. Some refer to dry flies with abnormally long hackles; others denote variants as dries with very small wings; still others as surface offerings with contrastingly colored hackle fibers or multicolored hackles. Spiders are often confused with variants, each having oversize but sparse hackle, a body, and a tail. There is a difference, though. Spiders are wingless, whereas variants usually have small inconspicuous spent wings. According to Harold H. Smedley's book, *Fly Patterns and Their Origins*, variants were first developed in England in 1875. But their popularity got a major boost in 1947 with Art Flick's fine book, *A Streamside Guide*. Flick also deals with direct imitations of individual natural flies, and I've found some of these effective as single imitations of several different hatches of May and stone flies.

Thus my early-season Gray Variant is basically a cross between the Dark Hendrickson and Quill Gordon, but the blue-gray hackle adds coloration of the Blue Dun and the Iron Blue Dun. When none of these flies is on the water I'm able to serve trout a reasonable facsimile of four flies which should be hatching during April and early May.

My Brown Variant, designed for use in midseason, symbolizes such well-known midseason flies as the March Brown, Ginger Quill, and Green Drake, the latter being a misnomer since the mature fly's body is often rusty white rather than green. Ginger Quill, being smaller, is not always as important when the larger flies mentioned above are on the water, but when they aren't, it's a must. As a result, I tied my Brown Variant on a No. 10 hook, compromising in size between the two larger flies and the smaller.

In late season the mountains bask in shimmering heat waves, and trout rise languidly for small May flies, aquatic midges, and terrestrial insects. Aquatic fly colors tend to be lighter; cream-yellows abound. There's the Light Cahill, and Pale Evening Dun May flies; also small yellow stone flies. For all, Art Flick's Cream Variant is an effective cross-section imitation. Important, too, is a dry rendition of that all-season favorite, the Leadwing Coachman. Flick's Dun Variant fits the bill perfectly. Tiny palmer-tied aquatic midge imitations (Nos. 16 and 20) are very useful in various colors (to be mentioned). This because the late-season color syndrome doesn't seem to apply with midges to the extent that it does with larger May flies. The fishing of terrestrial insect and aquatic midge imitations merits skill of its own and a fuller discussion later.

In Chapter 5 we discussed the stone fly (*Perla Capitata*) and above we mentioned smaller stone flies. *Perla Capitata* hatches on rocks, sticks, and tree trunks, rather than in water and is hence not so important as a dry as it is as a wet fly–nymph. But those other varieties of stone flies, as well as caddis flies, are sometimes important as dries. While trout do feed on them throughout the season, however, they do not constitute as succulent a diet as May flies, so we will not treat them extensively. Still, it's important that you be able to distinguish these two categories from May flies (Fig. 20).

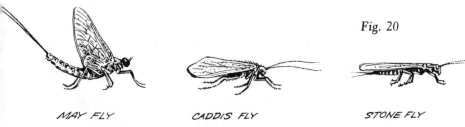

Fig. 20

MAY FLY              CADDIS FLY                    STONE FLY

Note that the horizontal wings of stone and caddis flies render their profiles more uniformly squat than that of May flies. An excellent imitation, in terms of profiles, is the bivisible dry fly, or a wingless, palmer-tied dry fly.

Developed about thirty years ago by the late Edward R. Hewitt, the bivisible constitutes a hook wound palmer-fashion with two or three hackle feathers. What with the fibers flared out in a 360-degree circle around the entire length of the hook's shank—and with no body—it's the best floater in the dry-fly family. Mr. Hewitt's bivisibles were usually brown, headed with a twist of white hackle. The fly, then, is as visible to fish as to fishermen—hence the name bivisible (Fig. 21).

SIZE 12

SIZE 20
(MIDGE IMITATION)

Fig. 21                    BIVISIBLE DRY FLIES
(ACTUAL SIZE)

Since they float so high and dry, bivisibles are very sensitive to riffled water, providing optimum bounce to the fraction of an ounce. Some fishermen believe that sunlight on the rebounding hackle fibers gives trout an impression of beating or buzzing wings, or of a surface-riding fly about to take off.

Bivisibles can be very handy when you find trout taking an unfamiliar fly type of any sort—May, stone, or caddis. Take note of the natural's size and coloration, then tie on your closest bivisible equivalent.

In addition to small bivisible midge imitations (sizes 16 to 20), you should have an assortment of larger ones, varying from 8 to 14—all in as wide a variety of colors as possible; black, furnace, cream, white, and grizzly will stand you 'in good stead when there's something hatching that defies more direct imitation. Keep in mind that you're mainly approximating size and color with bivisibles, so trout must not get too close a look. As with the wet fly–nymph, then, water should be used as an aid to obtain realism.

Fly life peculiar to low-water conditions—and the way to fish its imitations—constitutes discussion apart from the dry fly, hence its special treatment in Chapter 8. It will serve now to sum up dry-fly procedure as being as simple to master as it is exciting to experience when you hatch match by the season. Impressionistic variant dry flies and bivisibles make this possible. Beginners don't have to be entomologists; they can quickly gain confidence, and with it the experience to lead them into the matching of individual flies. The more experienced angler who can only get on a trout stream a few days each season—and who can't possibly know what kinds of fly hatches he'll meet—will find variants very helpful. He will be presenting imitations of what trout should be feeding on at that particular time, and since one variant can represent several different flies, it isn't necessary to carry many different patterns. A man with no flies other than those listed below could do a creditable job throughout an entire season. Here they are for your handy reference:

| GRAY VARIANT | BROWN VARIANT |
|---|---|
| early season | midseason |
| hook: 12 or 14 | hook: 10 |
| body: gray fur or wool, ribbed with peacock quill | body: brown fur or wool wound with peacock quill |
| hackle: blue dun mixed with black | hackle: mixed ginger and grizzly |
| tail: dun barbs | tail: cock pheasant fibers |
| | tying thread: olive silk |

## CREAM VARIANT

late season
hook: 12
body: light cock quill
hackle: cream color
tail: cream cock barbs
tying thread: primrose silk

## DUN VARIANT

all season
hook: 12
body: quill of red cock hackle
hackle: dark dun
tail: dun barbs
tying thread: olive silk

## MAY-FLY MIDGE

(SMALL BIVISIBLE)
late season
all colors, but a favorite is hook
   No. 18
body: none
hackle: either dark or light
tail: optional
tying thread: silk to match hackle
   color

## LARGE BIVISIBLE

all season
all sizes
all colors

Note: Variant ties are given for the convenience of your custom tyer.

Variants and bivisibles can serve as a bottom rung in the ladder of knowledge pertaining to fly life, a ladder that will lead you ever farther into the enchanting world of the surface fly.

# CHAPTER 7

# Tackle Tips for Fly Rodding

In progressing from farm pond to trout stream you have already acquired the basic equipment of the trout-fly angler. As most hobbies go, your outlay was modest —especially so because the more expensive items will last for years. What with the multitude of available accoutrements, it's easy to become a big spender, but you won't have to. My purpose here is fourfold: to suggest reasons for your basic equipment; to recommend additional equipment which improves techniques; to offer helpful tips as to its use; and to guide future purchases required for other forms of fly rodding. These will be covered in the remaining chapters. So this seems a likely place to review tackle.

## RODS

Most fly-rod instructors suggest that beginners use an 8- to 8½-foot rod. The reason given is that the longer the rod, the easier it is to keep line in the air. Ease of use varies little between a rod of 7 feet and one of 8, yet an extra foot can make a lot of difference on-stream when you're casting under and around tree cover. And that's why a 7- to 7½-foot rod will stand you in excellent stead on most trout streams.

You will hear a lot about rod action: trout, steelhead, and bass action. It's only necessary, though, to be aware of slow action and fast. Traditionally, the ideal wet-fly and streamer rod is a limber one. Its action, then, is slow, the better to impart pulsating movement to underwater flies. And since false casting is not as prevalent in wet-fly fishing as in dry, the stiff fast action of the classic dry-fly rod is unnecessary. But when you fish wet flies upstream, dead drift, there's no need for soft action. A tip fast enough for dry-fly delivery is just as convenient for the wet fly–nymph and a better casting instrument. And you can fish a mean streamer without an unduly soft action. A medium-action rod, then, is a satisfactory compromise for streamers, wets, and dries.

Ultralight (1 to 2 oz.) 5- to 6-foot midge rods have been gaining steadily in popularity since they were first developed about ten years ago. They make for especially challenging angling with heavy fish. Also, their extremely sensitive tips make it possible to fish the lightest of leaders (6 to 7X) necessary for tiny midges and terrestrial imitations (sizes 18 to 22). The tip action of heavier rods often snaps a light leader. These late-season flies are usually fished in dog days when vegetation is at its heaviest, and smaller streams are particularly hard to fish, even with a 7-foot rod. A midge rod is the perfect answer to many spots that are unaccessible to conventional fly rods. It's said that perfect timing is mandatory in casting midge rods, but anyone who is fairly proficient with those of more standard lengths will have no trouble with a midge.

Originally these little wands were available only in expensive bamboo cane. They are now sold in Fiberglas in a more modest range. For late-season fishing a midge rod is a must.

Since they are designed primarily for small dry flies, the action of all midge rods is fast.

When lake fishing for trout, bass, or pan fish you can manage well with your 7- or 7½-foot fly rod, but one of 8 to 9 feet is more satisfactory. Tree cover is rarely a problem, so a longer rod enables you to work more water with less effort. Also, long casts with short rods necessitate handling a lot of slack line; when you're seated in a boat this can be as vexing as it is tiring. As in stream fishing, on lakes each category of fly can be used: streamers, nymphs, wets, and dries. But most lake fishing calls for larger surface lures such as bass bugs, poppers, hair frogs, and mice; also deep-running small hardware like wet fly-spinner combinations and fly-rod spoons. The weight-and-air resistance of such lures requires heavier rods with backbone. Fast-rod action is also helpful for retrieving sinking line, often necessary on lakes when fish are deep down. Delicate manipulation of deep streamers or plastic worms, however, calls for slower, softer rod action, so your 8½- to 9-foot rod should have medium action, making it a common denominator for all lake situations. For salt-water ones, too.

Such a rod is ideal for all sea-run species of trout, including steelhead, salt-water battlers like bonefish, barracuda, tarpon, and many others. Angling for Atlantic salmon has come to be institutionalized to the point where tackle—from rod to flies —is in a class by itself. The rod norm is 9 or 10 feet of bamboo with a butt socket for a handle, inserted after a fish is hooked to facilitate playing him. Atlantic, like Pacific, salmon (chinook and coho), when sought on flies, can be taken effectively without extra-long rods with handles. Your glass 8- to 9-footer is very adequate.

A rod of the finest of cane will guarantee you no more fish than one of glass. Glass will serve you longer, will never develop a set (a warp), nor can it be easily broken by a fall, a car door, a destructive child, or a big fish. Thus, peace of mind is bought at low cost, plus the knowledge that it will serve well under all conditions you'll ever be likely to face with a fly rod.

By now it's probably manifest that I favor Fiberglas fly rods over those of bamboo cane. I don't for a lifetime of angling, for with a good bamboo rod comes something else: the warmth it suggests when fingered sitting by a fire, say, after a cold April Opening Day—warmth reminiscent of the sun-bathed cane fields from which it sprang. That amber patina on the stick helps conjure images of an unknown artisan lovingly coating the beautiful wand, perhaps wistfully hoping that the owner will be just as proud of it. You will love such a rod once fly-angling lore gets its grip on you, but give it time. First, drink deeply from the twin wells of on-stream experience and angling literature. Then the aesthetic appeal of a fine stick will grow on you, and with it respect, which leads to proper care. You will know when you're ready for one. In the meantime, stay with glass and permit peace of mind to help in improving your skill.

REELS

Your first 3¼-inch-diameter, single-action reel will be satisfactory under most conditions for your longest rod. But when you fish for large, long-running fish like steelhead and salmon, it's best to use a reel with more capacity. One 3⅞ inches in diameter will hold 100 feet of line and 30 feet of backing (rather than 100 feet of line and 100 feet of backing for the one of 3¼ inches). Backing is very handy when a large fish runs out all of your line. Such a reel also is ideal for salt-water long-runners, typical of which is the bonefish.

A midge rod requires the smallest reel available. A favorite is a diminutive Hardy Light Weight.

All three reels have single action with an on-off click and a drag. The click, when a fish makes his run, sings a wonderful song. To make the playing of heavy ocean fish easier, multiplying fly-rod reels are available, but they are necessarily heavier and more expensive.

LINES

The first fly lines were of horsehair; later they were made of silk, and oil-treated. When greased, silk line floated, after a fashion, and as it became saturated it grew heavier and heavier. They were not easy to handle, a reason, perhaps, for fly angling's being dubbed a pastime for experts only. But a dozen years ago this changed, with the advent of plastic-coated line extruded over a nylon core. Not only did this process make for vastly improved floating qualities, it permitted variations of thickness in given lengths of line; hence, uneven distributions of weight. A line could be built with a diameter that gradually expanded along its length and decreased near the end, streamlined like a torpedo. Such line shoots easily, making fly casting as simple as falling off a log, and greatly facilitates casting into wind and handling large heavy lures.

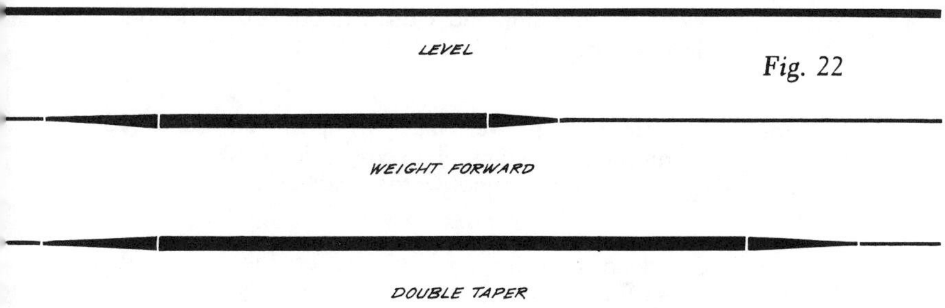

LEVEL

Fig. 22

WEIGHT FORWARD

DOUBLE TAPER

FLY LINES - TAPERS ARE EXAGGERATED

There are three basic tapers with which you should be familiar: the level, the weight forward (same as torpedo or rocket), and the double taper (Fig. 22). Previous to 1961, fly line was described by three-letter groupings such as HCF, GBF, HCH, referring to line diameters. These combinations can be confusing and they're hard to remember, so the American Fishing Tackle Association now classifies line by taper alphabetically, its weight in grains by numbers, and alphabetically again to denote specific gravity. DT9F, then, refers to a double-taper line of 240 grains (in the first 30 feet), floating. WF8S indicates a weight-forward line of 210 grains, sinking.

The chart below will enable you to familiarize yourself with this more convenient system. For example, you can immediately discover that for dry trout flies your 7½-foot rod should be fitted with DT5F line (double taper, 140 grains, floating). For deep-down nymph fishing it will take DT5S (same taper and weight, but sinking).

Now let's use the following chart to pair off your three fly rods with line required for situations described earlier and those coming in remaining chapters.

| ROD | CONDITIONS | LINE |
|---|---|---|
| 7½ foot | For farm ponds and small streams when winds are not stiff and more standard-size flies are used; i.e., sizes 8, 10, 12, 14. | Level or double taper |
| 7½ foot | Dry trout flies, wet flies, nymphs, and streamers on streams of average depth (3 to 6 feet) under normal water conditions. | DT5F |
| 7½ foot | On deep and/or high streams or lakes (when fish are deep), for nymphs, wet flys, and streamers. | DT5S |

| | | |
|---|---|---|
| 8½ foot | For lakes and rivers for bass and other warm-water game fish on the surface when using heavy and/or wind-resistant lures. | (Bug taper) WF8F |
| 8½ foot | When warm-water species are deep, on lakes and rivers and large or heavy sub-surface lures are used. | (Bug taper) WF8S |
| 8½ foot | When on large trout, salmon, or steelhead streams. | DT7F |
| 8½ foot | For large trout, salmon, or steelhead streams when fish are deep—particularly for winter steelhead. | DT7S |
| 8½ foot | For salt-water species fished for in shallow water. Note: special salt-water finish available. | (Bug taper) WF8F |
| 8½ foot | For salt-water species fished for deep. | (Bug taper) WF8S |
| 5 to 6 ft. midge | There will be few occasions for anything except WF or double-taper floating line as you will be using primarily dry flies, midges, and small terrestrials. | |

Properly cared for, a good fly line will last a half a dozen years of constant use. The only care required is the wiping of the utilized portion with line conditioner after use. A felt applicator is included with each can. At season's end, rewind your line to another reel, treating the entire length in the process.

In Chapter 1, I suggested that your line be tied to the looped butt end of the leader in any convenient knot. This is satisfactory for farm-pond beginnings, but as your presentation becomes more refined, you will discover that a knotted leader loop does not pass through smaller upper-rod guides as smoothly as does a nail-knot tie of line to unlooped leader. The leader's loop is snipped off and tied (Fig. 23).

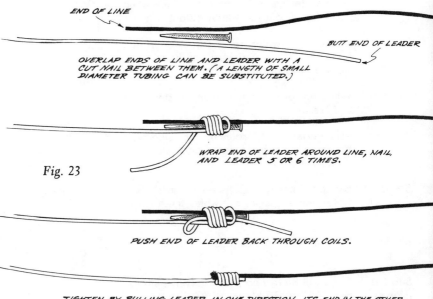

END OF LINE

OVERLAP ENDS OF LINE AND LEADER WITH A CUT NAIL BETWEEN THEM. (A LENGTH OF SMALL DIAMETER TUBING CAN BE SUBSTITUTED.)

BUTT END OF LEADER

WRAP END OF LEADER AROUND LINE, NAIL, AND LEADER 5 OR 6 TIMES.

Fig. 23

PUSH END OF LEADER BACK THROUGH COILS.

TIGHTEN BY PULLING LEADER IN ONE DIRECTION, ITS END IN THE OTHER. REMOVE NAIL, THEN TIGHTEN AGAIN. CUT OFF ENDS AND FRAY LINE END.

## LEADERS

Early leaders were made from horsehair, then from Spanish silkworm gut. The latter were brittle, unless well soaked. Present-day nylon leader is more efficient: it need not be soaked, doesn't tangle readily, and thanks to modern manufacturing methods, can be accurately tapered. Even more important, it is stronger than gut in the same diameters. So single-piece tapered leaders, suggested as basic in Chapter 2, are satisfactory under most stream conditions. Standard lengths are 7½ and 9 feet, and the packs are so marked, as is the size of the tippet, the last dozen or more inches to which the fly is attached. These sizes are denoted in X numbers; as the numbers ascend, the tippets decrease in diameter. For stream fishing for trout in the often high and roily water of early spring a 7½-foot leader tapered to 3X is satisfactory. When the water lowers and clears as the season progresses, longer leaders are needed to keep line from enlarged strike zones; and finer ones to preclude trout's spotting them. A 9½-foot leader tapered to 5 or 6X now is mandatory. The importance of fine leader in low clear water cannot be stressed too strongly. Expert casters, careless about leader lengths and tippets, often fail to take as many trout from a given stretch of low water as tyros who are leader-conscious.

These two basic leaders can be used on trout streams with the rods mentioned above, and on trout lakes and ponds as well. When fishing on lakes, be guided by the same rule of thumb. If water is choppy and clouded, 7½ feet of leader tapered to 3X will suffice. On clear and glassy surfaces use 9 feet, tapered to 5 or 6X. A word of warning: large flies will twist, tangle, and knot light-weight tippets.

When stream water is extremely low and bright, an extra-long fine leader with a small fly is often necessary, so it's beneficial to know how to tie your own leader. Differing sizes are available on plastic spools. The blood knot is used to tie one length of leader to another (Fig. 24). Leaders longer

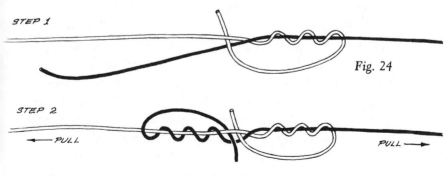

STEP 1

Fig. 24

STEP 2

PULL

PULL

TYING THE BLOOD KNOT

than 12 feet are difficult to handle unless there is a tail wing, so it's best not to exceed this length as a maximum, no matter what the size of your rod. Your leader segments should be stepped down so that the finished length will be evenly balanced. For example, if the butt end is heavy, 20-pound test, the middle light, about 10-pound test or 9/5 with a really light tippet (6X), the leader will turn over well in casting. (Note: Leader diameters thicker than 1X are graded in ascending order as follows: 1X, 0X, 9/5, 8/5, 7/5.) Twelve feet of low-water leader should be built with the Joe Brooks taper, as follows: 2 ft. of 25-pound test, 1½ ft. of 18-pound, 1 ft. of 6/5, 1 ft. of 8/5, 1½ ft. of 1X, 2½ ft. of 3X, 1½ ft. of 5X.

Under extreme low- and clear-water conditions, 6X and 7X tippets can be added to this leader.

When you're fly fishing for salmon and steelhead, the above leader guidelines apply, both for prepared leader and the hand-tied variety. Material is, of course, heavier throughout, the tippets usually ranging from 8/5 to 2X.

In salt-water fly fishing, tying is rarely necessary; for virtually all species, packs of about 30 feet of varying tests are available. Tapering is not so important for most ocean species and the emphasis is on test per pound. For example, a 10-pound-test leader is 10-pound tensile strength. Many salt-water game fish have extremely sharp teeth and/or gill flaps which can shear the toughest monofilament. Heavier shock tippets or even wire tippets are used as a safeguard. Space will not permit a rundown, by species and situation, of leader requirements based on pound-test. Your best bet for ocean fly rodding is to check with natives of the locale as to the right terminal tackle for the species you are most likely to encounter. Professional guides, charter boat captains, and sporting goods stores are invariably good sources of information.

Leader material for warm water is also graded by test per

pound. A 4- to 5-foot bugging leader, 3- to 6-pound test, is almost standard for bass, pickerel, crappie, and panfish, whether you're using a medium-size or longer fly rod. Some bugging leaders are tapered, but level ones are common for these unsophisticated battlers. Some fishermen pick their leaders to match the largest fish that can be encountered. If lunker largemouth of 6 pounds are common in a given spot, a 6-pounder-test bugging leader is appropriate. But a fish is buoyed by the water, and his pull does not reflect his entire weight, unless you horse him clear, which you should not attempt to do. Refined playing enables the finished angler to pit minimum leader test against maximum pounds. A 6-pound bass taken on a 1-pound-test leader proves one's mettle as an angler.

There's a tendency to equate pounds of test with the X system of measuring trout leader. Roughly, 2X equals 3-pound test; 3X, 2-pound, etcetera. Comparisons of this sort are inexact. It's a better idea to buy trout leader by the X number, and bugging and salt-water leader by test per pound.

CLOTHING

As I mentioned earlier, a good pair of waders or hip boots will last many a season if properly cared for. Immediately after use they should be hung inverted in a dry and preferably breezy spot. When storing, keep them free of dampness.

For wading big water and early spring's high water, chest-high waders are more convenient than hip boots. For low water and warmer weather, though, the less cumbersome boots make for easier hiking and less perspiration. While felt soles are more expensive, they're worth every cent. Felt helps to prevent falls occasioned by slippery moss and algae-coated rocks. Some prefer felt-soled wading shoes. These require stocking-foot boots or waders; their bottoms taper into sheaths, over which stockings are worn to protect the rubber or plastic sheath against cutting gravel which sometimes works into the shoe. In the heat of late-season wading, shoes are particularly convenient. Boots can be eliminated, and you can wade wet and cool with slacks. If streamside brambles and sharp-edge grass aren't too prevalent, swimming trunks are downright luxurious. Chains are also available for rubber boots. While they aid in preventing slipping, though, many find them bothersome to adjust.

During chill early-season days I strongly advise long underwear, heavy woolen hunting stockings, and a woolen hunting shirt. It's wise, also, to roll up and place in your back vest pocket a pull-over rain jacket. Those of light plastic are easy to fold and carry. Later on when the underwear is dispensed with, a long-sleeved cotton shirt replaces the wool one. Long sleeves protect against bugs and briars. Fishing caps should be well visored as protection against sun. Polaroid glasses are advisable. Besides cutting the glare, they're useful in spotting fish and protecting eyes from lashing branches.

One of the greatest contributions to the simplification of fly angling is the fishing vest. A typical one has four side pockets (one outer and one inner on each side), plus a large one encompassing most of the back, four acetate fly boxes affixed along the chest, a keeper for clippers, an attachment for your landing net, a wool patch for drying damp flies, and a zippered plastic creel. Given so much carrying capacity, compulsive collectors of angling knickknacks can load up like a Yankee peddler, but this unfortunate tendency reduces overall efficiency. The secret of getting full mileage from your vest lies in planned utilization of its capacity.

Each angler has his pet accessories. I only submit mine and my method of carrying them to guide your purchase of necessities and to inspire ideas as to their best use.

MISCELLANEOUS EQUIPMENT AND ITS USE

The list: fly book containing wet flies and streamers, fly box containing dry flies and nymphs, jar of leader- (and fly-) sinking fluid, jar of dry-fly floating fluid, container of slime-removing powder, knife, combination scale and measuring tape, collapsible drinking cup, stick of insect repellent, 2-inch-square piece of inner-tube rubber (leader straightener), and leader book.

This might seem a formidable list. It isn't when you store your vest sensibly. Let's say you're about to sally forth in ideal dry-fly weather. So as to have it immediately available, you put your box of dries in an outside pocket, along with the fly-conditioning powder and fly-floating fluid. It's warm and there are some cool pure springs along the stream. So in the other outside pocket you place your drinking cup and the leader straightener. Since bugs are rife, you include the insect repellent. The remaining articles are easily divided between the two inner pockets, for you probably won't need them for this outing. But you can't be sure. You might have to switch to wets, or streamerettes, and you'll have them in reserve. Also extra leader should you break the one on your line or wish to lengthen it. For that hoped-for trophy fish, there are always the scales and tape to keep you honest. The large pocket in the back is perfect for sandwiches and hooded rainshirt, even a camera.

Come wet-fly and streamer conditions and you fit out your jacket accordingly. Dries and their collaterals now go inside, in reserve, in case of an unexpected hatch. Systematized use of your fishing vest ensures against loss of its contents and promotes their effective handling.

A few words about this equipment. Fly books are wallet-like, lined in sheepskin. Since wet flies and streamers are flat in profile and made of supple materials, they're not harmed when pressed in a folding fly book. Being flat the book is very convenient for carrying. The stiff hackle of dry flies and the fine antennae of nymphs must be better protected, however, and fly boxes are the answer.

There are boxes of many sizes and shapes. Most are of aluminum, lined with clamps in both bottom and lid. Some are divided into compartments with glassine snap covers. One compartment can be opened while others remain closed to guard against fitful breezes. I've found the clamps unhandy because push and pull is sometimes needed to get delicate flies attached and withdrawn. The compartments are better, but my favorite for twenty years has been one of the magnetized variety. Only 2 x 4¼ inches, it has five magnetic projections to keep over fifty-odd flies from falling out or blowing away. I place them in groupings and am spared time in rummaging around for what I want. I've never had occasion to wish this easy-to-carry little box any larger. For those who do feel constrained to carry more flies, however, there's always the group of acetate boxes in your vest.

Sinking fluid is spread on the leader and wet fly (or nymph) when you have trouble getting them deep enough. It's useful, too, when fishing dry on low water and you want to make certain that your leader is immersed and not floating. There's no surer way to spook fish than to have leader riding high, especially when it lies partially coiled. Coiling can be eliminated by squeezing the rubber piece against the leader and pulling its entire length through the gripped rubber, taking care that not so much pressure is applied as to break it.

Floating fluid is applied to the dry fly before you begin fishing. The more you false cast, the longer its effectiveness lasts. When the fly begins to ride low, squeeze water from the hackles and put on another application. When you take a fish, the slime from his mouth will clog the hackle fibers. Pour out a bit of fly-conditioning powder in your palm, rub the fly in it, then remove powder by blowing and using the little brush on the container's cap. Apply floating fluid, and false cast a few times. Your fly will float perfectly.

The two best floating fluids that I know of are Mucilin and DuBois "Up." The only slime-removing powder that I've been able to locate is DuBois "Fly Dry." It's a tremendous boon in avoiding the changing of dry flies after one or two fish are taken.

I've found the DuBois leader book the most convenient of all. It's of leather and contains plastic sheaths that pivot singly on a grommet. Each sheath is trimmed in a different color, which can be used as identification markers to denote leader sizes.

Should you choose to clean fish on the stream or examine stomach contents by way of ascertaining the trout's current food, you'll need a knife. A good one to get is one with a whetstone on the handle. Hook points of flies that are fished deep are prone to wear dull on rocky bottoms. Nymph strikes being as weak as they usually are, it pays to present the sharpest of hooks when nymph fishing. An occasional sharpening on one of these knife handles keeps hooks at top efficiency. As mentioned, much of this equipment can last a lifetime, and since he usually buys as he progresses, the outlay rarely pinches the average developing fly angler—unless he permits it to by going overboard in one or a couple of fell swoops.

# CHAPTER 8

# Between the Hatches

There are times during perfect dry-fly weather when fly hatches are insignificant and fish are disinterested, even in those seasonal surface imitations which should score well. The logical answer is to fish wet. For underwater nymphs are always prevalent as ready food. But let's suppose that you have long awaited a day of dry-fly fishing. You're determined on a real college try before surrendering to wets. What to do?

## ATTRACTOR DRY FLIES

Like bass (but not to so great a degree) well-fed or disinterested trout can sometimes be goaded into striking. One of the best flies with which to rile them up is a spider dry fly—a fly with hackle fibers of exaggerated length (Fig. 25).

These unusually long fibers help to skitter the fly across, and even against, the current. Instead of picking up your spider at the completion of its drift, allow it to sweep into a dragging action. Then lift the rod tip and jump the fly across the surface. That trout are attracted rather than duped by skittering is proved by the vicious strikes which often result.

Fig. 25

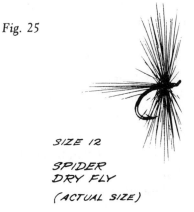

SIZE 12

SPIDER
DRY FLY
(ACTUAL SIZE)

Sometimes a brightly colored attractor pattern such as a dry Fan Wing Royal Coachman or a George Harvey Fish Finder will get similar results at times when a proper deceiver won't work. Their more conventional hackle fibers rule out skittering, but even in free float, attractor dries often evoke terrific wallops, possibly because they anger the trout. While these lures are foreign in terms of color, their silhouette is familiar. This, I am thoroughly convinced, is the only way to explain my success over many years with a dry Fan Wing Royal Coachman when what should produce won't. But remember such phenomena are the exception. At times of limited hatching activity be sure to follow the rule calling for thorough fishing of seasonal imitations before resorting to attractor dry flies.

MIDGE DRY FLIES

Between-the-hatch situations are more likely to obtain in late season when May-fly activity tapers off. Second only to low water, dwindling hatches are responsible for keeping many fly anglers off the stream. This is a pity, for trout do keep feeding; indeed, more voraciously than earlier, when the

pickings are heavier. A prime food is the midge. So great a
variety of miniscule aquatic *Diptera* (midges) are continuously active as to preclude their being noted as specific
hatches. Actually, they're so small that many anglers don't
notice them—let alone try to imitate them. An important fact
often forgotten is that trout don't get a much better look at
the tiny midge than the angler does. To be sure, you can't
imitate the tiniest of midges, but go down to a size 20 or 22
tied palmer, and the riffled surface will make the size differen-
tial almost academic. In fact, the fish must be more eager than
usual lest these most difficult to locate of all flies bounce out
of reach.

It's easy to spot a midge situation. Imagine you get on
stream during a midsummer afternoon when trout are surface
feeding everywhere. A cursory glance, however, reveals no
flies. Study the small eddies and water-lapped bases of boulders, though, and you will discover the source of the rise—
tiny flies often cream or white in color but sometimes darker,
floating or at rest on the boulders and dipping up and down
near the surface. In riffled glides the trout slash fiercely; quiet
flats show more deliberate rises. Here a trout will sometimes
arch completely clear for airborne midges, easily visible
through his crystal canopy. Your leader will be just as visible,
and, as you have learned, this is water to steer clear of. Rather,
go for those riffle-feeders. The regular hot spots should be
sought out and fished as before. The odds are heavy that you
will have a thrilling afternoon, and should you fish into the
evening, the action will very probably improve. For now you
can handle those quiet flats with less danger of leader-
spooking.

You will find midges no more difficult to fish than more
standard-size dry flies, but two precautions must be taken:
since water is usually lower than normal when midges

abound, stand as far away from your fishing area as possible. At least 9 feet of leader tapered to 6X, or even 7X, is now mandatory in order to get your fly to pay-water effectively.

Apprehension about handling long fine leader and tiny flies causes many an angler to pass up midges and the excellent results they can provide. True, a heavy rod's action can easily snap fine leader, but a midge rod will lessen the possibility. Remember, too, that anyone who can handle 7 feet of leader can cope with 9. A little backyard practice will quickly instill confidence.

True, too, is the fact that small flies are pesky things to tie to a 6X leader. One answer is to tie several midges to leaders before you go out. If one is lost, or should you wish to change colors, just change leaders. You can also get a magnifying glass to carry on the stream. The most useful sort is a jeweler's loop. Held over the eye by your squinting action, it leaves both hands free for tying.

TERRESTRIAL DRY FLIES

Sometimes attractor dry flies and midges fail to turn the trick on hatchless days. Sure-fire fallbacks are terrestrial insect imitations. Ordinarily, the use of terrestrials is as misunderstood as their effectiveness is unappreciated.

Small terrestrial flies were the brain children of Vincent Marinaro and Charles K. Fox. Their experiments on the limestone Letort in central Pennsylvania led to Marinaro's classic, A Modern Dry Fly Code, its theme being that lush, pastoral limestone locales produce an abundance of land-bred insects which afford trout a major source of food. This fact had been largely unrecognized because most terrestrial insects are infinitesimal: the tiniest of beetles, ants, leaf rollers, and jassids. Marinaro described his imitations and the manner of fishing them. Expertise unlimited is required, for the Letort's stream-bred brown trout are as worldly wise as fish can be. Small wonder, for their domain runs through well-trafficked back yards and pasture land, where lumbering cattle cause unsettling bankside tremors. Smooth diamond-clear water permits these trout long and critical looks at drifting food, so imitations must approach perfection. Their presentation among the naturals on which trout are feeding (fishing the rise) demands casting of the highest order. The leader should light like thistledown, the lure's drift must be letter-perfect, for the trout will rarely budge from his feeding station. When a Letort lunker takes, steely nerves are required to cope with his dynamic lunges against a 1½-ounce rod and 6X leader.

Thus was born the cult of the Letort whose devotees symbolized the ultimate in fly-rodding finesse. Little wonder that terrestrial technique came to be misinterpreted. Literature equated it with tough-to-fish limestone waters, but the ratio of limestone to freestone streams in North America is extremely small, so the average trout fisherman, largely restricted to upland streams, tends to dismiss terrestrial fishing as being almost a foreign art form, pursued by virtuosos only.

But terrestrial insects are important edibles for mountain trout—primarily from mid- to late summer, as terrestrial populations peak and May-fly hatches decline. The terrestrial's deadly effectiveness on broken mountain water is widely unappreciated, and so is the ease with which they can be fished. Actually, many anglers fish terrestrials without realizing it.

When fish and flies aren't moving, a thunderstorm can be a welcome development, so don't make the mistake of quitting. Even if you're driven from the stream, get back on it as soon as rain abates, and fish the biggest of dry flies, numbers 4 and 6. The answer: wind and rain sweep all sorts of land insects from overhanging foliage to the surface. The largest—moths, crickets, bees, grasshoppers, and oversize beetles—are easiest for trout to spot. When the elements provide a feast in times of relative famine, fish aren't too choosy, and the wide range of available terrestrials precludes the necessity of imitating a single species. So any large dry fly (preferably of deer hair) represents a good cross-section of different large insects. Deer-hair flies are excellent floaters, and they have the coarse appearance of most large terrestrial insects, as opposed to the more delicate configuration of May flies. Always have a few for hatchless days that turn gusty.

Even without benefit of gusts, enough grasshoppers fall in streams to render them recognized fare to trout. The lowly grasshopper, then, is due a specific imitation. Hoppers are often used as fallback lures, fished on bright summer water when nothing else works. This makes sense for nothing is so apt to interest a somnolent trout as that large mouthful. But the larger it is, the better it had better look on that super-clear water. The closer an artificial hopper resembles a natural, then, the more effective it will be.

The deadliness of hoppers as a between-the-hatch expedient was well demonstrated in July, 1967, by John Stauffer, with whom I was discussing this chapter. Fishing had been as dull as the day was bright; during bankside conversation I ventured that we could use a storm. John said that maybe we didn't need one. He was staring at a grasshopper resting on the toe of his right boot. He caught it and flipped it to the water. After a short drift, it vanished in a slurping swirl.

I had no hopper dupes with me, and John had only two, both exquisite imitations in size 6. On his first cast to the chummed fish John scored, a 9-inch brown. We worked upstream, taking fish in quick succession, over forty in an hour on three-quarters of a mile of stream. The largest was a 14-inch brown. He nailed my hopper as it tumbled off a tuft of grass overhanging a bankside cut. Action was ended by loss of my hopper in a tree and John's hopper disappearing in the jaws of a trout.

John claimed this was the "damnedest between-the-hatch action" he'd ever seen. I was about to agree when he cut me off brightly with a valuable afterthought. "Title that terrestrial chapter 'Between the Hatches,' " he said, "to emphasize the fact that this is the time to fish, not to quit!"

We've seen how his point was borne out by large terrestrial imitations in general and grasshoppers in particular. If these lures are effective sometimes, tiny terrestrials are murderous all summer. They're so small as to deny trout close scrutiny, especially in turbulent freestone streams, as opposed to slow limestone water. And like grasshoppers, which are more prevalent and hence more effective in some locales than others, these miniscule jassids, beetles, and ants are everywhere (Fig. 26).

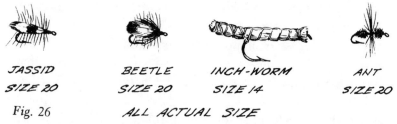

JASSID          BEETLE        INCH-WORM           ANT
SIZE 20         SIZE 20        SIZE 14          SIZE 20

Fig. 26        ALL ACTUAL SIZE

It's easy to determine when to fish the smallest terrestrials. You will remember that midge feeding is signaled by rises the stream over. Except for small streams completely arbored by trees, terrestrial rises are more prone to be along the banks. Unlike the well-distributed aquatic midges, terrestrial insects can only get to water from land and overhanging foliage. Witness my phony hopper tumbling off that overhung grass into the jaws of the nice brownie. For every real grasshopper that tumbles off the bank, there are myriads of smaller landlubber insects. It takes many to dent a trout's appetite, so when May flies are scarce and fish aren't rising to midges, you will often find consistent rising along shorelines.

Sometimes close observation results in a match. In June, 1967, I joined a beginning angler friend who had been on the stream an hour earlier. He was fishless but greatly excited. Pointing to a hemlock surrounded by rhododendron on the far bank, he exclaimed, "There's a trout trying to climb that tree!"

One seemed to be doing just that. Every half minute or so a nice brown tail walked beneath the overhanging greenery. A quick look at bankside foliage was sufficient to reveal tent caterpillars, undulating up and down over the water on their gossamer filaments. We moved cautiously across the stream, perhaps twenty-five feet below the tree-climbing fish. I tied my only caterpillar imitation to my friend's leader. On his third cast he snagged the trout—a spectacular foot-long fighter whose arching leaps and long runs led him a merry chase over slippery watermelon-size boulders. I never saw a happier angler, the more so because his brown fell for a matching phony. But the ending was not so auspicious, and, since there's a lesson to learn, it bears mentioning.

It turned out that my partner had a caterpillar in his box which he gave to me. But whoever tied it put in weight. It was awkward to cast and quickly sank out of sight. A few fish struck while it was near the top, but I missed them. Finally it was snagged and lost on the bottom. Then the other was lost in shrubbery. I bailed my friend out by clipping down a Grizzly King wet fly to its green body. He took two fish, and then lost the thing in a tree. Try as we mightily did, trout would touch nothing else. I still curse the character who tied that caterpillar with lead, a stupid thing to do because—as was borne out by that tree-climbing fish—trout take caterpillars on top, not on the bottom. The moral: make sure that your caterpillars are as light as feathers, and from midspring until midsummer always have three or four in your fly box.

When you don't see bankside rises, small terrestrials are still a very safe bet. If enough naturals aren't in the water to occasion visible rises, you can be certain that they have been there fairly consistently throughout the summer and that they will be again. Trout are familiar with them then—particularly ants, both the winged variety and common crawlers in differing colors. Exact imitations of ants—as well as tiny beetles and jassids—are not nearly so important on freestone water as on limestone.

I once fished a stream on which there was a veritable plague of small cinnamon-colored beetles. My closest imitation was a brown ant, size 20. Trout went after it as eagerly as they did after the natural beetles, so I was greatly chagrined when I lost the brown ant in a large fish. It was the only thing in my box resembling those cinnamon beetles, but a black ant worked just as well. I experimented with a red ant and a white one. All scored as well as the brown.

The answer was simple: that rough water provided erratic lure action. As we found with midges, trout had to strike before the tiny ants were carried away. In rough water the ants' color and shape were harder for trout to detect than their size.

The ants were so small that trout couldn't be too particular. And very important, since terrestrial season brings with it such a wide variety of minute insects that it was natural for trout to take my ant even if it did not look like a beetle, for ants were prevalent at the same time. It's seldom necessary, then, to match individual insects (the tent caterpillars were an exception) when terrestrial fishing on freestone water—a great boon to the beginning fly fisherman.

Minute ants and beetle imitations do not ride high on the water, but float in its surface film. They are presented exactly like dry flies, though; and when fishing the water instead of the rise, the tedious presentation common to limestone terrestrial fishing is eliminated. There is no need for careful calculation of the lure's float by way of placing it so that it will glide accurately into a waiting fish's mouth. The riffles, rather than the angler, direct the decoy into channels of fish's natural food, so pick your water as you would when dry-fly fishing, and let it do the work for you.

This land-bred small stuff, then, is the deadliest between-the-hatch bait available, and contrary to popular belief the easiest to fish, so long as you stick to riffled freestone water. It's a pity that terrestrials have become synonymous with tougher-to-fish limestone streams. It's unfortunate, too, that so many anglers quit trout fishing after the major May-fly hatches are finished, for this is just when terrestrials are the most deadly.

If you lose fish because of the breaking of light leader, don't be upset. For light leader is the key to optimum action. In the end, the more action, the more fish.

# CHAPTER 9

# Warm-Water Fly Rodding

Some of my fondest boyhood memories are of a gleaming New Hampshire lake, a jolting fly rod, and hurtling smallmouth bass, each of whose gaping maws was festooned with a Mickey Finn streamer. The lake is still very productive, but today the prescription for smallmouth is different. You can fish for days without spotting a fly fisherman. Spin fishing has taken over.

Such is the case with warm-water game fish everywhere. Bass, pickerel, pike, crappie, and bluegills—excellent fly-rod fish all—are now sought almost exclusively with spinning rigs, the growing popularity of which is attributed to their being easier to use than fly rods and more effective. Longer casts and retrieves make for more effortless coverage of more water. Casting accuracy is more easily achieved. Large lures (often necessary for bass) can be cast as readily as small ones. Plainly, when compared to spinning, fly rodding seems too much like work.

The advantages of spinning over fly casting cannot be denied, but it's easy to exaggerate them. Many fishermen do, and they miss thrills second to none. More's the pity, for warm-water game fish are more accessible the country over than trout. The seasons are generally longer, for one thing, so no matter where you live, you're assured of virtually year-round fly fishing. More important to the beginning fly angler, warm-water species are easier to take on flies than trout, especially bass, because of their willingness to strike almost any lure. This permits the angler to spend his valuable time hooking and playing fish rather than coaxing them to strike, as is so often the case with trout. The tyro fly rodder is thus afforded experience from which he can develop fly-rod know-how for use over the more difficult trout. It can be an exciting experience: the superb fighting qualities of bass are magnified by the light weight of a fly rod and its whiplike action. No wonder that his first fly-rod bass is cause for many a spin fisherman to reassess the merits of his original rig. I've known some who never went back to spinning.

The purpose of this chapter is to correct some popular misconceptions about warm-water fly rodding—particularly as they relate to bass—and to enable you to take the work out of this exciting form of fly angling.

LURE PRESENTATION

Many fishermen associate fly fishing for bass with surface lures only. Even the largest fly-rod deer-hair bugs, flies, frogs, and mice are light enough to be easily delivered by the heavier line. As a matter of fact, underwater fly-rod lures are often too heavy for effective casting. Also, spoons, tandem fly spinners, and plastic worms are prone to snag on stumps and weeds prevalent in largemouth habitats and sometimes on rocks in smallmouth water. Too many equate bass behavior with that of trout, only using fly rods when bass are rising. As a result, the relatively few who still fly fish for bass usually use dries only, relegating subsurface lures to spinning rods which cast them better and afford more backbone for the punishment that comes from underwater snagging.

It should be remembered, however, that bass are not like trout; they are more prone to strike out of anger than from hunger. Thus, more often than trout, bass can be goaded into rising, and there's rarely the need for discriminating insect imitations, let alone the matching of specific hatches. There are always exceptions, however. I've run into heavy dragonfly hatches on largemouth lakes and found a sparse-dressed deer-hair imitation of the natural's size to be the only effective lure, but such exceptions are few. Most of the time you can fish surface lures for bass very successfully when none is working on top. This is particularly true of the largemouth, thanks to their particular habitat.

As was noted on farm ponds, ideal largemouth feeding water is shallow—the better for trapping food. Weed beds, lily-pad-clogged flats, and stump-infested shoals are sure hot spots, as they usually range from a few inches to a foot or two in depth. So surface lures and deep runners appear the same to bass, there being very little distance for them to rise.

Largemouth bass, then, can be fished for with fly-rod surface lures most of the time, and it is not a complicated form of fly fishing at all. As opposed to the obstacle-ridden tree-covered alleys that are most trout streams—lakes, ponds, and rivers permit easy and relaxed casting, for impediments are not around and over the fishing area. Rather, they're in the water itself, so stumps, weed beds, and patches of lily pads become targets for casting, not hindrances.

Effective casts to largemouth are ensured by taking plenty of time. Many trout anglers, accustomed to quick line pickups occasioned by fast water, instinctively fish lakes too hurriedly. They expend unnecessary effort and catch less fish. In making

conscious effort to extend time between casts, you will en-
hance opportunities for strikes and take the work out of fly
casting. Five minutes between the lure's touchdown and
pickup is not excessive.

Let's say you're fishing a hair frog around lily pads. The
frog is dropped as close to the pads as possible. It should float
for a minute or two, then a slight twitch can be imparted. For
another couple of minutes the frog floats motionlessly, then
it's twitched again and floated until the pickup.

Watch a frog basking in warm shallows. For long minutes
he lies absolutely still, then he sometimes moves a short distance or perhaps swims away from the area. This is the action
you are simulating. All the while a meanly disposed bigmouth
may be watching, and often he won't take until the poor crit-
ter has made a move or two. I've seen this happen on my own
farm pond over many years, sometimes with a hair frog,
sometimes with the real McCoy.

Bass bugs and flies should be kept on the water as long as
frog imitations, but it's wise to activate them more, as would
be the case, say, with a fallen and struggling bug or moth.
While you're imitating natural phenomena, exact duplication
as to anatomy and color is not so important with bass as with
trout. As noted, bass aren't choosy; realistic action seems to
be the key to success, for such tends to attract and madden
the fish.

Locate these largemouth feeding stations and concentrate
on them. Don't waste time on open water with no apparent
cover to afford bass a sense of protection as well as food.
Once you've chosen your spots, there's rarely need for long
casts. A quietly paddled canoe or skiff can get you within
thirty or forty feet of the target without putting down fish.

Smallmouth require like presentation; however, they are
more generally distributed throughout the northern reaches of

the continent where lakes and rivers are cooler and less sub-ject to growth or vegetation. Prime smallmouth water is clear, gravel-bottomed, interspersed with sand bars, scattered with partially submerged piles of boulders and lined with rocky outcroppings and shelves. Here smallmouth seek protection and food, so casts should be directed accordingly and fol-lowed by protracted waits, punctuated with the lure manipu-lation prescribed for largemouth. Even in deep water, small-mouth are easily lured to the top, often when there's a dearth of surface feeding, for clear water ensures maximum visibil-ity. Once they spot the lure—even though it may be some distance away—chances for rising are good, for smallmouth are among the freest-rising fish of all, quicker to respond and more agile than their more ponderous largemouth cousins.

When it's tough to coax them topside, smallmouth are very easily sought in the depths. Thanks to those sand and gravel bottoms, snagging becomes less of a problem than in more heavily vegetated largemouth water. As mentioned, I cut my teeth on fly rodding with smallmouth and Mickey Finn buck-tails, and I have yet to find a readier taker of flies, from top to bottom, than this most spectacular of battlers, the smallmouth bass. So never pass up a chance to fly fish for him, and don't demean him with spinning or casting rigs.

There are times when largemouth, too, are hard to coax surfaceward. Abnormally warm or cold water is often respon-sible, and either condition makes them sluggish. Underwater lures now become necessary, and contrary to accepted dogma, they can be fished easily and effectively, obstructions notwithstanding. Undeniably, most underwater fly-rod lures, being heavy and wind-resistant, are unwieldy to cast. The answer is to reduce casting. I hit on a simple and deadly method of doing so years ago on a small lake in North Caro-lina.

Unfastening a rented rowboat from its owner's half-submerged wharf was a tricky business. Preoccupied with avoiding a ducking, I neglected the business end of my line, which trailed overboard with a fly-rod plug. After a few minutes of jockeying the boat toward midlake, I spotted a slowly unwinding coil of line on the floor boards. I reeled up the slack, placed my fly rod on the seat and went back to rowing. Hypnotized by the pine-scented surroundings, I wasn't aware that more than a few feet of line were out until the rod clattered towards the back seat. I lunged for it, just in time. Far to the rear in a shimmering burst of white water a catapulting largemouth hung instantaneously against blue sky, his flanks glistening in bright sunlight. A resonant fallback marked him for a lunker, but I never knew for sure for he threw the plug on the second jump. Still, I didn't regret the loss, for the experience suggested a method that is simple to master and very effective.

When fishing fly-rod plugs and underwater lures, I maneuver to the windward end of lakes, allowing breezes to drift the boat and troll the lure. Still fishing would be a better description, for usually the boat drifts slowly. Its movement is sufficient to pay out slack, however, so casting is reduced to a bare minimum. It's only necessary for concentrating on especially fishy-looking hot spots which a lazy drift-by might not cover thoroughly. The only "work" involved is an occasional twitch of the rod to simulate the intermittent struggling of an injured minnow or the fitful swimming of a frog. Long slow drifts allow lures to cover more water in less time than is possible through casting. The maximum number of fish see the lure. Small wonder, then, that action is consistent and electrifying, thanks to the superior flexibility and light weight of fly rods.

The slow-lure movement resulting from drift-trolling prevents a snagged hook from being as deeply imbedded in a stump as it could be if the lure were one rapidly propelled. Also, when movement is slow, a snag can be better felt as it develops. A few careful twitches can often free the hook.

In water so clogged with obstacles as to preclude drift-trolling, the most effective way to prevent fouling is to fish smaller patches of water (the fishiest-looking) in a vertical, rather than a lateral, manner, a method known as jigging. Your lure is allowed to sink to the bottom; very slowly, it is manipulated straight up. In reasonably clear water a large streamer's teasing action can be visible to a lot of bass. In cloudy water a sure killer is a wet fly-spinner (or streamer) combination; the turning spinner blade reflects what light there is for optimum visibility.

Weedless-hook lures are very helpful in underwater prospecting for largemouth, but confidence that they won't snag should not lead to their being fished too rapidly. When any fish is sluggish, he won't react to fast-moving lures. Proof of this and of the superiority of fly rods for deep, sluggish bass was well demonstrated a few years ago when I was fishing a pond on Maryland's Eastern Shore with the local fish warden and a couple of friends.

Largemouth were deep and very slow-moving. The chill October weather was probably responsible, for by late afternoon the ferocity of strikes was declining in direct proportion to the falling water temperature. Since nothing could be done with bass along the shoreline, we went after them in the middle of the pond, on the bottom, with spin-casting tackle and plastic worms. Although we hooked fish regularly, many were lost because of the weak striking.

So it came as no surprise when one of the group lost a whopper. A few minutes later his boatmate also yelled something about missing a fish in the same spot. It was in deep water opposite a concrete drainage pipe on the shore.

The warden oared our boat into the area. He laid down an on-the-mark cast and allowed his plastic worm to sink all the way. He had retrieved only a foot or two when his rod buckled wildly. In seconds it snapped straight. The fish was gone. The warden noted that he hit so lightly that it was hard to determine whether he was hooked.

I tried, with the same results. We drifted away, and the other boat moved in. The fish was hooked but lost almost immediately.

Before our next turn was due, I asked the warden for one of the small brass rings that he slips on plastic worms for weight; I wanted that worm in the strike zone fast! Shortly after the warden missed the fish again, I connected. A few frantic bulldogging rushes followed. Then he broke loose. The other's turn was due, so we moved on. Each of them missed the fish again.

Thinking that my 4-ounce fly rod (rigged) might telegraph those weak bumps better than a 7½-ounce spin-casting rod (rigged) I quickly switched, so quickly that I neglected to put on a smaller fly-rod worm. I noticed that the brass sinker band had come off. On so light a rod the worm constituted more weight, anyway, than I liked to handle, so I dispersed with a new sinker.

The fish met my worm halfway down. Through the fly rod his bumps felt more like thumps. I kept the worm moving up, temptingly. As if concerned that his food might escape him, the fish struck harder, but still not solidly enough for secure hooking.

Now my worm was visible, undulating only inches beneath the surface. Below it we glimpsed hazily a flash of olive-green.

I grabbed the feather-weight fly rod in both hands, the better to check a premature jerk which would have ended the contest. For the worm had reached the surface. Then it disappeared in a blinding splash. After a long struggle that can only be described as vicious, the warden netted my 5½-pound largemouth. He grasped the fish while I removed the well-chewed plastic worm. Far back in his jaw I saw a golden glitter. Mystified, I asked that the fish be tilted head down. That little brass ring rattled to the floorboards.

I certainly don't attribute this victory solely to the superior sensitivity of my fly rod. Casting rigs might have done in the bass eventually, but the fact remains that they hadn't after nine consecutive tries. I'm convinced that earlier use of the fly rod would have ensured the landing of at least some of those lazily striking bass that escaped.

What with their sensitivity to weak strikes, fly rods are invaluable in crappie fishing. While he's a strong fighter, the crappie tends to take lightly, and has a soft mouth. Heavy rods and lures often result in hooks being torn loose and lost fish. The best approach to crappie fishing is to troll a streamer from your fly rod while oaring or drifting slowly. Those light bumps are easily detected, and a light strike on your part usually affords secure hooking.

The northern pike are seldom considered a fly-rod fish, possibly because they're often deep feeders and usually deep fighters. Still, they can be raised, particularly in shoreline shallows and amidst sand bars. The northerns' surface strike is downright frightening. The most dramatic fly fishing I ever experienced was on Canada's Lake of the Woods water near Minaki, Ontario, where northerns abound. In early morning and evening they took murderously from the top. In midday they went for deep-trolled streamers. Two bamboo rods were smashed, due to my nervous inexperience with this vicious cannibal battler of the North.

LURE SELECTION

Fly-rod surface lures are legion. Besides the hair flies, bugs, frogs, and mice mentioned above there are many varieties of "poppers," most with cork or plastic bodies; some are plain and others fixed with hair wings. Poppers usually have concave heads, and when jerked along the surface water are scooped up snowplow fashion. The effect is a gurgling sound calculated to annoy and raise bass. Since angering bass is so often the key to raising them, some fly-rod poppers should be an integral part of your warm-water kit. Pick up a dozen in differing sizes, colors, and styles, but be sure to have duplicates of your deer-hair imitations. As was pointed out, these lures have deceiving as well as attracting qualities when used in the habitat of their natural prototypes. For example, abandoned water-filled quarries are often excellent producers of bass. Field mice sometimes tumble off their sheer walls. Hair mice, played along the edges of quarries, have been proven by many the most effective quarry lures of all. (Fig. 27).

*Fig. 27*

The easiest to use of all subsurface fly-rod lures is the streamer. All sizes will cast nicely; even large streamers don't have too much wind resistance—particularly when wet and matted down—and their action is murderous. Not only do they look and move like small fish, but that undulating movement of hair or feathers excites the killer instinct of all warm-water, as well as cold-water, species.

The angler can add weight to streamers to suit his gear and

to facilitate fast sinking. This can be done by winding lead foil around the leader where it is tied to the streamer. Split shot can also be used. Custom tyers can be instructed to work foil into the bodies of streamers, but the best bet is a reserve reel with sinking line.

Good for smallmouth is the Mickey Finn, Black-Nose Dace, Little Rainbow Trout, and Gray Ghost (sizes 6 or 8). These same patterns work well for largemouth, but since big fish like big mouthfuls (largemouth generally grow larger than smallmouth) your sizes should be 4 or 6. The same holds true for pickerel and northern pike. An excellent large streamer is a 4-inch White Maribu on a size 4 hook. Its big fluffy feathers can be made to breathe convincingly by the slightest movement of the rod.

An excellent lure for all warm-water game fish is a large nymph, preferably an imitation of the dragon-fly nymph. Weighted and fished slowly up from the bottom, large nymphs are deadly in the extreme (Fig. 28).

*Fig. 28*

DRAGON-FLY NYMPH IMITATION

When fish are feeding actively but deep down, nothing beats gaudily colored small-size spoons and plugs, typical of which are fly-rod-size Trix-orenos and Flatfishes. When fish are deep and slow, the best possible lure is the plastic worm, fly-rod size, slowly trolled.

Rid yourself of misconceptions and learn to take the work out of it, and you will find warm-water fly rodding a most exciting and productive method of taking fish.

# CHAPTER 10

# Salt-Water Fly Rodding

If warm-water lakes, impoundments, and rivers perform as safety valves in channeling growing fishing pressure from diminishing areas of cold water, the ocean's diverting potential is like that of gigantic floodgates. Off the coast from Labrador south to the Florida Keys, and from the Gulf of Mexico north through British Columbia, lie roughly nine thousand miles of unspoiled water. Its character varies as widely as the many species of sport fish it supports. Bays, inlets, and estuaries provide scenic backdrops comparable to the loveliest of fresh-water locales, and as interesting. Current-breaking reefs, shifting sand bars, pilings and jetties present water-reading situations that are especially challenging, for the ebb and flow of tides render their character changeable. Finally, there are feeder rivers, streams, creeks, and canals, at first brackish, later fresh; repositories of salt-water species as well as sea-run fresh-water battlers that range far inland to spawn, sometimes in the very streams, and even stream sections, where they were born.

It might seem proper to discuss sea-run (anadromous)

fish under fresh water, as most are generally equated with fresh-water fly rodding, but many can be taken from the ocean on flies. Runs are particularly heavy in saline estuaries, prior to being blocked by dams or decimated by commercial fishermen and pollution, so your potential for action with most migratory game fish is greater in salt water than in fresh, sufficient reason to treat them here.

### SEA RUNNERS

The Atlantic salmon deserves his well-touted reputation as king of game fish. His great size (40 pounds is not uncommon) and exquisitely proportioned, silvery body, coupled with a proclivity for sizzling runs punctuated by soaring leaps make him a worthy candidate for the crown. He clinches it by being as capricious as a trout, but much more majestic in his rise. It's safe to say that the surface take of the Atlantic salmon is the most thrilling moment in all fly angling; it can also be a dangerously deceptive take.

In early fall Atlantic salmon cruise the rivers of northeastern Canada and Maine to their headwaters. There they spawn, after tarrying along the way to rest in long slack-water stretches, often a mile in length. The most productive of these "salmon pools" abound in the beautiful rivers of Canada's Maritime Provinces. Some are leased by provincial governments to individuals, who may form private clubs or run commercial fishing camps. Others are privately owned. All are restricted to fly fishing only.

The supposed dearth of open water deters many anglers from attempting northeastern salmon fishing, and the aura of exclusiveness surrounding this splendid fish discourages more, especially those who consider themselves novices. Woeful misunderstandings these. A year in advance of a trip, contact the fish and game departments in the capitals of Canadian Maritime Provinces and the state of Maine, and you will find that reasonably priced, comfortable accommodations are available. In fact, there are areas of open water in the Maritimes, mostly in the estuaries; and while there are millionaires' pools, there are also some excellent ones within the reach of any fly angler dogged enough to track them down.

The real trick in taking Atlantic salmon is to hit the run at its peak. Persistent extracting of on-the-spot information is the answer. Meet the run in water that's not too high or too low, and the odds are good that you'll land at least a grilse (not over 5 pounds, a young salmon)—and you'll probably get your hook into something at least twice that big. In some circles it's heresy to say that hooking salmon is easy, but it is when the conditions are right. I discovered this as a rank novice on New Brunswick's Miramachi River.

The wide smooth flow was devoid of the obstructions to casting so common to most trout streams. My guide (who went with the camp) instructed me in classic wet-fly salmon technique—downstream quartering, as recommended earlier for streamers. Strikes, called "takes" by salmon fishermen, usually coming as the sunken fly swung into its quartering action, were contiguous with long rapid runs during which line was completely surrendered. As far as 100 yards away, runs ended in towering leaps. Then came the reeling, while fish came along, until constrained to take off again. Again, line was released by the click of the single-action reel until another high jump signaled a repeat retrieve. The process was continued until the salmon tired sufficiently to be led head-first into my guide's long-handled net.

I soon learned to beach played-out salmon by leading them into shoreline shallows or gravel bars. You can also clasp them at the fore of their tails and lift them clear. Tail landing is easier, however, when Lee Wulff's tailing device is employed.

When a salmon takes, your first impulse is to strike immediately. Resist the urge, as you might pull the fly away from him. Chances are that he'll hook himself. To play safe, strike when the fish is felt, not when it is seen, thus the hook is embedded before that first run and jump. When the jump comes, your rod tip is lowered, so the weight of the fish does not crash down on a taut leader. But when he has fallen back, it must be tightened again, quickly, so that hook-retaining pressure is maintained.

In a general way, dry flies are presented to Atlantic salmon much as they are to trout. But in low clear water, it is a common practice to cast straight across and even quartering downstream so the leader does not drift over the fish ahead of the fly.

Real effort must be exerted to resist striking before the take, a supreme effort since the majestic rise to the fly is in full view before the fish actually has the fly. The sight of a gigantic fish slow-rolling toward your fly is conducive to instinctive striking, but the fly must not be budged until loose line rolls from the free hand. Then the strike is in order.

While suggested fly patterns for sea-run and salt-water fish are included at the end of the chapter, we should note here that attractor patterns only are used for Atlantic salmon. This is because on their way to spawn salmon feed very sparingly, if at all. They take artificial flies out of anger or inquisitiveness. This is not to suggest, however, that salmon are not sometimes selective. I remember very well a fly tied with wool from a guide's sweater that worked mayhem when nothing else interested them. The right fly is found by trial and error and the persistent questioning of other anglers, should the camp owner and his guides be stumped. Usually they aren't. By far the most economical approach to Atlantic salmon fishing is two to three weeks spent in the Maritime area, including Newfoundland. Devote a week to salmon and the remainder of the time to fishing coastal inlets and backwaters for sea-run brook trout. Fresh from the sea, these very gamey fish sport flanks that are more silvery than the more brightly mottled landlocked varieties. Sea-run brookies are also more prone to surface fighting—even to clearing the water, the exception rather than the rule with fresh-water brookies. Generally, sea runners are unselective. Bright, classical wet-fly patterns are most effective. In shallows, during long summer evenings, however, they will rise readily to any kind of dry flies.

This is fishing easy to come by. The water is usually open and rental skiffs and canoes are plentiful. My most enjoyable sea-run brook trout fishing has been on Prince Edward Island. The many inlets afford a maximum of fish and a minimum of fishermen. But there are always boys, knowledgeable as to the best spots, who are happy to row for a dollar or two a day.

Presentation is the same as that described in Chapter 9 for warm-water lakes. So is tackle (see chart on page 80–81). While an extra reel with sinking line is sometimes handy, I find floating line generally satisfactory since casting to and drift-trolling over the shallow areas of tidal inlets and creeks is my favorite method. Your 8- to 9-foot rod is more convenient than a smaller one for reasons outlined in Chapter 9. Also, since this can be your salmon rod as well, it's only necessary to pack one rod for a Maritime trip. Parenthetically, beginning salmon anglers often find it easier to play these big strong fish on salmon rods. Camps usually have them to lend, but do try your lighter fly rod before you leave.

From northeastern coastal waters to those of the central

portion of the Atlantic seaboard the American or white shad
(unlike Atlantic salmon, there are none in Europe) is prized
as much for his fighting ability as his succulence. This deep-
girthed, silvery sea runner might well be termed the poor-
man's-salmon, for his spawning runs are heaviest where popu-
lation is most dense—principally in the Connecticut, Dela-
ware, Susquehanna, and Potomac rivers. While the shad
offers excellent potential for fly rodding, most anglers don't
seem aware of the fact, possibly because the use of shad jigs
with spinning rods has become so popular as to be accepted as
standard tackle. But as early as the 1930's anglers were taking
shad on flies, both from boats and by wading shorelines of
rivers and shallow tidal flats of estuaries.

In the Susquehanna, Tom Loving of Baltimore, John
Stauffer's teacher, was a pioneer with a killing fly having a
black wool, silver-ribbed body and a white bucktail wing on a
3/0 double hook. Their approach was that of the nymph
angler—the upstream sink-and-draw method. Strikes usually
come as the fly begins its upward ascent. Proof of the worth of
this technique is borne out by the success of the spin fisherman's jigging procedure. A jig is dropped overboard and allowed to sink to the bottom. Then it's reeled up a foot or two
and is activated only by the pitching action of the boat. On
the Susquehanna, jigging is so deadly that it has surpassed
trolling in popularity. If you can hit a shad run in shallow
flats, wading and sink-and-draw fly casting can produce exciting action. But when shad are moving in deeper channels,
orthodox fly fishing is difficult to come by. My favorite
method is fly-rod jigging as described in the last chapter, but
with regular shad jigs. They sink faster than flies and once
down, they undulate, attract, and catch shad as well as they
do on spinning rigs. The fact that these lead darts are too
heavy for effective casting is of no moment since you won't be

casting anyway. Troll them until you locate a school, then begin jigging. A 4- to 6-pound shad on a fly rod will give you one of the best fights you'll get, so don't fail to meet the next shad run with fly tackle. If you live anywhere along the New England or mid- to South Atlantic seaboard, your trip can be short in time and inexpensive. While not as fine as table fare, the smaller hickory shad is also a splendid battler. He's common to the same waters as the larger white shad. Hickory runs are particularly heavy in southern rivers. Southern shad runs occur in November and December; mid- and North Atlantic seaboard runs are in early spring when the dogwood is in bloom.

Also along the Atlantic seaboard (and well into its southern reaches), the hard-fighting striped bass will prove a worthy candidate for your fly rod. Like the shad, he is seldom sought with fly tackle, a real pity because he takes flies—particularly streamers and surface poppers—very readily. Possessed of a tougher mouth than the shad, he's easier to hang on to if, that is, you can outlast his violent runs and thrashing turns. Also, at all levels he's a heavy feeder so it's not so necessary to plumb the depths as you often must for shad, which, like salmon, feed very little on spawning runs. Standard quartering of your streamer against the flow in estuaries, bays, and rivers (where the stripers spawn) gets excellent results. The wading of flats when the tide is out is a popular method, so is slow trolling, drift trolling, and bass-bug casting, after a school has been located. However, the largest striped bass don't school as commonly as do smaller ones. Your best bet for a 20-pound lunker is trolling. One of these savages on your 8- to 9-foot fly rod will prove a never-to-be-forgotten experience. What with the capacity of this fish for lightninglike, long, straight-away runs, never fish for him with less than 150 yards of backing behind your salt-water fly line. While the shad's runs tend to be more circular, it's best to have an equal amount of backing for him, as well, to be on the safe side.

The striped bass is also plentiful along the Pacific Coast. So is the shad, which was transplanted from the East. Eastern methods of taking both fish on fly tackle serve equally well in the West.

A few worldly wise anglers recognized Pacific Coast salmon as marvelous fly-rod fish shortly after large-scale settlement of the Pacific Northwest, but the Atlantic salmon's gamey cousins are only now beginning to come into their own. Even today, however, the vast majority of Pacific salmon, principally the huge chinook, or king, and the smaller coho, or silver, taken by anglers are fought on deep-sea or spinning rods. The common bait denominator is chopped herring. Along the coasts of Oregon, Washington, and British Columbia, there are scores of vacation villages catering to salmon fishermen. Pacific salmon are sought by parties of about a half dozen from chartered cabin cruisers. If a fly angler gets on one of these boats, he'll quickly find that he's a less than welcome member of the party, for the captain knows that the play of a salmon on a fly rod—under the boat and around it—necessitates withdrawal of his bait-fishing clientele's lines for extended periods. I found this out the hard way by wasting an entire day on one of those charter boats. After a motorboating fly angler was located, I had an exciting time with my 8½-foot wand and some high-leaping cohos.

Motorboating is almost the universal method of taking cohos and chinooks on fly rods, and a prime area is Puget Sound. Large streamers are trolled rapidly (about 5 miles per hour for cohos, 2 miles per hour for chinooks) 50 feet behind the boat's wake. The strikes are violent and the fish usually hook themselves. But as a dash begins, a precautionary strike from the angler is in order. Fights of an hour are not uncommon with 10-pound cohos; up to four or five hours with 20- or 30-pound chinooks. Their swift long dashes require at least 150 to 200 yards of backing.

As on the East Coast, complete information in advance of a salmon trip is a must, but in the Pacific Northwest it pays to contact individuals in the know about fly fishing rather than tourist bureaus and state conservation departments. So foreign to the area is the fly rod for salmon that your only safe sources of information are the several outfitting houses. Norm Thompson Company of 1805 N.W. Thurman, Portland, Oregon, 97209, was the one that so kindly bailed me out. I strongly urge anyone contemplating West Coast fly fishing of any kind to contact the firm's president, Peter Alport, or one of his staff well in advance of planning a trip.

A singular blessing bestowed on fly anglers by this region's beautiful waters is year-round fishing. Salmon are on their spawning runs from mid- to late summer into late fall. In winter and spring, steelhead (sea-run rainbows) work into the same coves and rivers to spawn. And throughout the entire year cutthroat trout (cousins of eastern brookies) run back and forth to the sea, not just to spawn. The cutthroat is possessed of a wanderlust exceeding his annual call to reproduce, so you can take this superb fish almost any time.

As with salmon, the preponderance of steelhead and cutthroat are taken on bait, mostly salmon eggs with spinning and deep-sea rods. The relatively tiny fly-angling fraternity usually troll deep streamers in estuaries and the wider rivers. Wadable rivers and streams are usually quartered with large brightly dressed wet flies and streamers. As a general rule, boat fishing should be conducted as on fresh-water lakes. Stream fishing calls for the standard streamer approach. Since winter and early spring sea-run trout are usually bottomhuggers, sinking line is often more effective than floating. Occasionally, when they're found in shallows, they can be raised by a large dry fly. But such instances are uncommon.

## FLY FISHING THE OCEAN

Many ocean game fish that are willing to take flies cruise coastlines, bays, inlets, and saline inland waterways, often the same water inhabited by anadromous species prior to their upstream migration to fresh water. Salt-water species can be taken inshore on the same fly tackle used for sea runners entering coastal areas. Some variations in equipment, however, can be helpful.

Many ocean fish have razor-sharp teeth and gill flaps. A 6- to 12-inch stainless-steel wire leader is good insurance in extreme southern and tropical waters where leader-rippers abound. Also a multiplying fly reel loaded with monofilament and a casting-head fly line aids fly anglers when they tie into really big fish, say, a 100-pound tarpon. It's easier to cope with such brutes with a fast-winding reel—especially when they're heading at you and slack must be brought in quickly. Techniques, too, are the same as those employed for sea runners, namely, motorboat trolling, drift trolling, casting from boats, and wading.

Those hundreds of miles of tidal marshes and creeks from the northern through the mid-Atlantic seaboard afford ocean species as fit for fly rods as the best of the sea runners. Usually different species are at their peaks at different times, so the angler must stake out a native or two and keep in close touch. For when word comes that "the weakfish are in" or "blues are running," he must be ready to move quickly.

The weakfish may not be the sea's most pugnacious fighter, but he does love flies, any kind. When he's in shallows he'll rise to dries. Mostly, however, any kind of bright bucktail is

the best producer. He's attracted by a progressively swift retrieve, either directly against the flow, quartered into it, or in
slack water along weed beds. He's named for his weak mouth,
so he must be played with care.

The bluefish will take flies with the alacrity of the weakfish,
but he's much more the spectacular battler and wild jumper.
Small blues inhabit inshore waters and most run from 6 to 12
inches. Some may reach 5 pounds. Other excellent fly-rod fish
are mackerel and pollock. While they, too, can be taken inshore, they are essentially offshore fish, as are larger bluefish,
some of which reach 25 pounds.

The most effective approach to offshore fly rodding is trolling. As on fresh-water lakes, maximum water coverage enables lures to be shown to the greatest number of fish. Thus
when they're not schooled, you have the best opportunity to
pick up singles. But singles aren't your goal; in the ocean you
should seek schools. Trolling enables you to do this. When
strikes come fast, you can be certain that a school has been
struck. The motor should then be idled and the area slowly
circled while casts are made into the center of the school.

A choice method of school seeking is bird watching. Spot a
concentration of diving gulls and terns, and you can be pretty
sure that surface-feeding fish are at work. Practically all salt-
water game fish—particularly mackerel and blues—will rip
into gatherings of fry fish, driving them surfaceward, where
hungry birds await them and their sliced-up remains. Sometimes acres of water are aboil. Any kind of streamer or bucktail cast into the maelstrom will furnish the most furious and
arm-wearying fly fishing that you will ever encounter.

Another method of locating schools is chumming. Chopped
shrimp or herring spread on the surface will often bring a
school up to where it can be worked over with streamers.

But even the thrills inherent in mid-seaboard fly fishing

pale when you get your first taste of stunning action on glittering, azure-green flats surrounding the Florida Keys and in the mangrove-studded coves dotting both coast lines and the Gulf of Mexico. This is truly the new frontier of American saltwater fly fishing. In these pristine reaches the fly angler can match stamina and wits against infinite quantities of numerous species of game fish. In the flats of the Keys, bonefish, permit, channel bass, ladyfish, jack crevalle, and barracuda require stamina equal to or exceeding that demanded by the strongest of fresh-water, sea-run, or ocean fish. But the demands on one's nerves—the need for accurate casting and patience in playing—make Keys fly angling as entrancing and challenging an experience as can be found anywhere.

Shallows around the Keys are generally approached with powerboats, to which skiffs are attached. On sighting fish an angler and his guide (or companion) repair to their skiff and move cautiously toward the school. It's easily seen. In water from several inches to a foot or two in depth, protruding backs, dorsal fins, or tails are sometimes visible. A large concentration of channel bass (also known as redfish) will often create a continuously moving swell, clouded by mud (when it's prevalent in bottom sediment) agitated by nose-nudgings of the fish. When channel bass and bonefish scrounge the bottom for food fish, their tails protrude, undulating in flashing sunlight like the sails of an advancing armada. This can be unnerving for the angler as he waits for the fish to get into safe casting range, from 50 to never less than 30 feet, in the case of the wary bonefish. Often the angler will dismount from the skiff and wade toward the school.

The fly must never be dropped smack in a congregation of the bonefish. Rather, a single fish, or a few close together, should be aimed at. The fly must drop lightly several feet to the fore of the target, then it is moved in short stabs of in-

Fig. 29

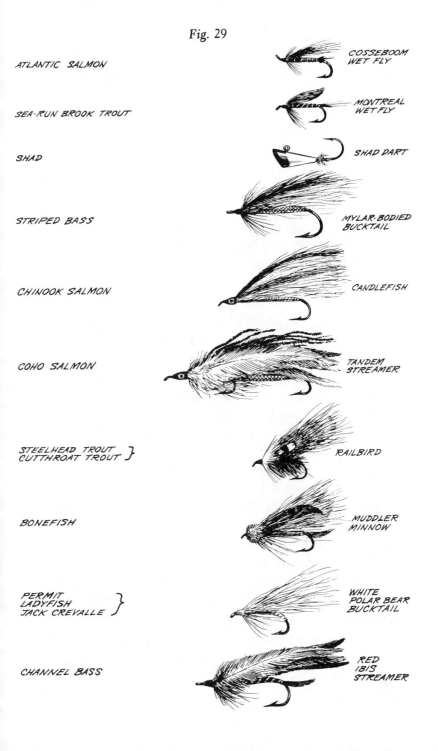

ATLANTIC SALMON

COSSEBOOM
WET FLY

SEA-RUN BROOK TROUT

MONTREAL
WET FLY

SHAD

SHAD DART

STRIPED BASS

MYLAR-BODIED
BUCKTAIL

CHINOOK SALMON

CANDLEFISH

COHO SALMON

TANDEM
STREAMER

STEELHEAD TROUT
CUTTHROAT TROUT }

RAILBIRD

BONEFISH

MUDDLER
MINNOW

PERMIT
LADYFISH
JACK CREVALLE }

WHITE
POLAR BEAR
BUCKTAIL

CHANNEL BASS

RED
IBIS
STREAMER

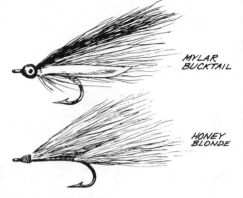

BARRACUDA

MYLAR BUCKTAIL

TARPON SNOOK

HONEY BLONDE

creasing velocity away from the fish. If he moves for the fly but stops, fly action can be decreased for a few seconds, then started again. More often than not, a chilling strike follows. Then comes a frightening run, back through the school, which scatters in a flash. After the fish is caught, or lost, a new school must be found.

Presentation to the channel bass need not be so painstaking. His bad eyesight enables you to work closer. The fly should be placed as near to his nose as possible. Other game fish of the Keys and Coastal waters such as ladyfish, barracuda, jack crevalle, and permit also require careful placement of the fly. This is most true of the permit. Few of these violent fighters are taken, but they are regarded by some as being, pound for pound, the best fighting fish of all. They represent, perhaps, the biggest challenge of all to fly anglers of the fabulous Florida Keys.

All of these fish, with the exception of the permit, are ready takers of brightly colored bucktails, and most will rise to surface bass bugs and poppers, as will those spectacular brawlers of mangrove swamps, the tarpon and the snook. These, too, are flighty fish, but more is required than prudent presentation. A mangrove covers the surface, and roots beneath it make for obstacle fishing second to none. No matter how adept an angler may be at casting to and checking the mad runs of snook up to 25 pounds and tarpon of over 100, more fish will be lost than landed. But the challenge that is mangrove fly fishing is such that an opportunity to sample these exotic waters should never be passed up.

Offshore fly fishing procedure along Florida and the Gulf Coast is like that in the mid-Atlantic area in all respects save chumming methods. Snappers, pompano, mullet, spotted sea trout and that prime fly-rod fish, the dolphin, often get too deep for surface chumming. Deep-sunken chumming lines, baited with small fish, are slowly retrieved by way of bringing the quarry topside. Once they're up, they can be cast to with any kind of salt-water bucktails and even surface poppers.

These same offshore fish can be pursued in like manner around the Gulf of California and up the West Coast. There is, of course, no hard and fast line of demarcation between what constitutes offshore and inshore species. Some of the fish denoted here as offshore feeders do work close to beaches and even into inlets—the spotted sea trout, for example. And inshore species are sometimes taken well beyond the breakers. My purpose here is to suggest general guidelines for seeking those multitudes of ocean fish which will take a fly. There are, of course, others; space will not permit treating them all. It's no exaggeration to say that there are species yet to be discovered as fit prospects for fly tackle. Possibilities for the expansion of salt-water fly rodding, then, are so great that all this chapter can do is suggest the possibilities. Still, it is to be hoped that your appetite has been whetted sufficiently to inspire you to wet a salt-water fly. But the overriding purpose of the chapter is to stress that you need not be an expert to tackle salt-water fly rodding. The know-how already gained on fresh water will serve you well—if your nerves are good.

**CHAPTER 11**

# Ten Commandments of
# Stream Etiquette

Implicit in a civilization's development is increasing awareness of manners. This is especially true in sports, whether the competition is between man and man or man and animal. In the latter case—fox hunting, for example —dictates of good form sometimes become extremely complicated, but, surprisingly, rules of etiquette are not generally equated with angling. This will probably continue to be the case until angling is defined as a pastime rather than a sport, for sport connotes competition, and fishing is more than just a contest in killing fish. When more anglers become less obsessed with competing against each other and concentrate more on matching wits with their quarry, angling etiquette may evolve more rapidly. This will bode well for the future of the ancient and honorable tradition of fly fishing.

Even in the most exalted angling circles you will hear references to someone "out-fishing" someone else. This is unfortunate, for anglers absorbed solely in outwitting their quarry become skillful faster, and very quickly their self-confidence precludes competing with other fishermen. So the First Commandment of angling etiquette should be to compete with fish, not other anglers.

The Second Commandment hinges on the first: only kill fish (particularly trout) when there is good reason to do so. Conservation organizations emblazon streamside trees with posters reminding anglers that they'll catch more fish if they kill less. "Catch and Release" stretches are dedicated to this proposition. I suggested in the Introduction, dwindling trout habitats and burgeoning numbers of fishermen dictate the need for the adoption of the "catch and release" philosophy by all who fish for trout with flies. The urgings of interested organizations in the name of conservation will help, but real progress won't be made until the killing of trout as a yardstick of success is considered a breach of angling etiquette.

There are times when exceptions to the rule can and, in some cases, should be made. Deeply hooked fish are often unharmed when the leader is snipped and the fish is released with the hook still embedded. His enzymes will eventually rot out the hook. But if a fish bleeds profusely, chances are it will die, so it might as well be creeled. When you're fortunate enough to land a trophy trout (one in the 18- or 20-inch range) you should feel free to kill it, for such trout sometimes become cannibalistic and prey on smaller populations. Also, a really big trout can be considered the ultimate in success, so an angler deserves to keep him. When you're camping in a wilderness area with myriads of wild fish, some for the skillet can be condoned, and a few nice trout for a host with whom you're staying, or for a gourmet friend, are perfectly in order. It is this angler's opinion that a person who measures the success of his outing by the weight of his creel is, at best, unenlightened.

It was noted that there is a connection between competing and fish killing. The beginning fly angler sometimes kills fish to prove to his companions—or those at home—that he actually can catch fish. This is only human. Most, if not all of us, who cast flies for trout have gone through this stage, and sometimes it's hard to get out of it.

My father, whose fishing experiences encompassed his boyhood (worms and sunfish), harbors secret misgivings about my fly-fishing abilities. I can tell from the slightly quizzical, half-peeved look that often follows my rejoinder, "released 'em," to his invariable request for "a few trout," on my returns from outings. I've tried to lay low his disbelief, and now and again I do produce a few.

Chances are good that you will come to greatly value fishing for enjoyment rather than meat. You will have become part of a fraternity that elevates the catching of fish to an art form; one with unparalleled literature and tradition—tradition which you are helping to preserve by releasing your catches. You should be proud, too, in enabling the hope of our patron saint, Theodore Gordon, to become a reality. Almost a half century ago in describing a stream restricted to flies (an oddity then) he wrote, "Such a law as this would be of great benefit to all trout streams. . . ." As Charles K. Fox says in his *Rising Trout*, "Theodore Gordon fathered and championed the concept of fishing for sport as opposed to meat. He sold to many the idea of putting them back alive, something the English weren't doing."

The Third Commandment of stream etiquette proscribes "horning in." Often it's unintentional, but anglers should guard against moving into water soon to be fished by someone already on-stream. Scout the area for others. Either fish behind another party or get well ahead. When the next man reaches your starting point, sufficient time should have elapsed to permit the fish to settle down.

Commandment Four follows logically: cut your wading to

a minimum. Only do so to facilitate casting. When possible, use dry rocks as steppingstones. You won't disturb water for those behind, and you'll be easier on subsurface fly larvae.

Commandment Five contributes to optimum enjoyment when you're fishing with a companion. Give him the opportunity to fish alone. He might find you charming company, but he might also enjoy solitary communion with the stream. If he wants to stay with you, give him equal opportunity to fish the best spots. This is easily accomplished by taking turns by the stretch. As you move along a stream the hot spots tend to even out between you.

Excitement often results in an angler's breaking Commandment Six. When action is heavy at a given spot, it's easy to spend a lot of time fishing it. Of course, if no one is waiting, stay on, but it's not good form to hog good water when others are on the stream.

Also, if you're fishing in front of another angler, it's best to take no more than a couple of fish from one pool (or distinguishable spot). It might be that there are only a few fish in that area. A trout that's felt the hook can be fly-shy for days. Judgment must be used, however; if a pool is large, a couple more might be snagged without putting down the majority of fish in it. But Commandment Seven, two fish to a pool, is a good rule of thumb to stick to.

Spinning gear has its places, but one of them is not a proper trout stream. When one fine stream, previously restricted to fly gear, was opened to spinning, it was speedily denuded of a fine head of native trout. Spinning is that deadly, so it's outlawed on most good club streams. One, on which I've fished in the Poconos, is so anxious to preserve its stream-bred browns that anyone caught with spinning tackle is drummed out and never allowed to return—be he a member or a guest. So Commandment Eight calls for fly rods on trout streams.

Commandment Nine will seem so obvious as to preclude mention, but many who should know better sometimes break it through thoughtlessness. Don't litter a trout stream. Nothing mars the beauty of an arbored mountain stream more than cast-off food wrappers, bottles, and cans.

Last summer I was shooting action pictures with Ed Murphy, senior editor of *Sports Afield* on a gem of a Pocono mountain stream. Under a hemlock overhanging a beaver pool, Ed's dry Cahill was gobbled by a 14-inch stream-bred brown trout. I had little time to check the area prior to shooting the spectacular action. We noticed the beer can only after Ed's fish was netted and hoped fervently that it wouldn't show. But on each color transparency the half-sunken can, hard against a gnarled root of the hemlock, was jarringly obvious.

Commandment Ten is automatically acknowledged by those of good breeding—the first time. I suggest that it be adhered to repeatedly. When an appreciative angler is permitted to fish private water, he usually offers something to the owner by way of appreciation. Often, though, hospitality is taken for granted by the recipient and appreciative gestures fall away with the years. I'm one of the few guests permitted to fish a native brook trout stream in the Poconos simply because I sent a box of chocolates for the Christmas following my first visit and continued doing so for fifteen years.

By honoring these Ten Commandments of stream etiquette you will increase your enjoyment astream and your companion's and serve to perpetuate the pastime, through your practice of trout conservation and by the example you set for others. You will become a better angler; indeed a better person—one with whom the shades of bygone giants like Walton and Cotton, Maryatt and Halford, Hewitt and La Branche could enjoy a summer evening.

**CHAPTER 12**

# A Fly Angler's Library

The next best thing to fishing is thinking about it, or talking about it, or both. The well-read angler reflects vividly on his pastime. And usually fishes better than poorly-read anglers, too. The more you read about fishing, the greater will be your enjoyment, on-stream and off.

Angling literature informs, provides vicarious pleasure, and encourages erudition. The earliest mention of fishing in English writing, one "Colloquy No. 53" of Archbishop Aelfric, in A.D. 1000, contains "how to" information; so does Dame Juliana Berners's "Treatise of Fysshynge Whyth an Angle" in the mid-fifteenth century *Boke of St. Albans*, generally accepted as the first writing on artificial flies. Izaak Walton and his collaborator, Charles Cotton, went further; while instructing they proselytized. "Having once practiced . . . then doubt not but angling will prove to be so pleasant that it will prove like virtue, a reward to itself," wrote Walton in his *Compleat Angler*. Reveling in the excitement and good fellowship inherent in angling, he savored pastoral splendor in prose of the highest order.

Many writings since Walton's have been directed toward the same end. Some have succeeded admirably as blends of know-how and adventure; others are stronger on information than adventure, or the other way around.

A beginning student of fly-angling literature is well advised to start with books on general information before moving on to more specialized works. Books can serve as benchmarks of improving stream generalship. It's regrettable that space won't permit a longer chapter, because each category has many fine books. But this chapter will suggest a systematic approach to your reading and collecting.

The collecting of fishing books does not pose much of a problem. Well-run book stores can be of some help. But your best bet is to get on the mailing lists of companies that publish catalogs of fly-fishing equipment. Most of these companies also handle angling books. An excellent source of out-of-print volumes is The Anglers' and Shooters' Bookshelf, Colonel Henry A. Siegel, Goshen, Connecticut 06756.

A good place to start is with your quarry. Some interesting ichthyologically oriented books are *The Scientific Angler*, Paul C. Johnson; *Through the Fish's Eye*, Mark Sosin and John Clark; *The Ways of Trout* (When Trout Feed—and Why), Leonard Wright, Jr.; and W. B. Willers's *Trout Biology: An Angler's Guide*.

By way of sharpening up your on-stream techniques and gaining an overview of fly fishing, I strongly recommend the following books: *Fly Casting with Lefty Kreh, Practical Fishing Knots*, Lefty Kreh and Mark Sosin, and *Art Flick's New Streamside Guide to Naturals and Their Imitations*. The Flick book is short enough for you to read in one evening. It's so easy to understand that even if you have no previous exposure to fly life you can become immediately engrossed in the subject. It serves as an admirable first step toward tackling more advanced texts. Included in this group should be two excellent general-information books: the old Ray Bergman classic, *Trout*, and a contemporary work that represents an ideal step up, *Joe Humphreys's Trout Tactics*.

There are many other general-information books on fly fishing for trout. Notwithstanding differing treatments by their authors, these volumes pretty much plow the same ground. So if they're read back to back to the exclusion of adventure, literary masterpieces, and books on individual facets of the pastime, your interest might flag.

General writings are more useful and enjoyable when added to your library over an extended period. Space allows me to mention only a few that have stood the test of time: Tom McNally's *Fly Fishing*, A. J. McClane's *Practical Fly Fisherman*, John Atherton's *The Fly and the Fish*, Joe Brooks's *The Complete Book of Fly Fishing*, Richard Talleur's *Fly Fishing for Trout*, and Dr. Alvin R. Grove's *The Lure and Lore of Trout Fishing*.

These books cover practically all facets of the sport, but others focus on specific facets. Of particular interest are books about the trout's food: namely, forage fish and—more particularly—insect life.

For many years, the bible of streamer fishing has been Colonel Joe Bates's *Streamer Fly Tying and Fishing*, and the same author wrote *Streamers and Bucktails—The Big Fish Flies*. Beautifully illustrated with color plates of a very wide range of patterns, these books cover all aspects of streamer fishing. Beginning fly anglers, in particular, are well advised to read Bates because streamers are often regarded as good "beginner flies." A group of baitfish imitations that have proved highly successful for many streamer devotees were popularized by designer Keith Fulsher in *Tying and Fishing the Thunder Creek Series*. This is an important book for streamer fishermen.

The watery world of nymphs has brought on a plethora of

writings in recent years. A few that should prove interesting and helpful to you are: *The Art of Tying the Wet Fly and Fishing the Flymph*, V. S. Hidy (James Leisenring); *How to Take Trout on Wet Flies and Nymphs*, Ray Ovington; *Tying and Fishing the Fuzzy Nymphs*, E. H. (Polly) Rosborough; *The Masters on the Nymph*, J. M. Migel and L. M. Wright; *Nymphing*, Gary Borger; *Nymph Fishing for Larger Trout*, Charles E. Brooks; *Nymphs*, Ernest Schwiebert; *Soft-Hackled Fly*, Sylvester Nemes; and *Dave Whitlock's Guide to Aquatic Trout Foods*, Dave Whitlock.

Two of the most innovative angler-writers on the contemporary scene are Carl Richards and Doug Swisher. The Swisher-Richards team's acute observations and inventiveness have led to the relatively recent popularization of upstream wet-fly/nymph fishing through the medium of their emerger and stillborn nymph patterns. In *Selective Trout* and *Fly Fishing Strategy*, Swisher-Richards expound these and dry-fly theories in a compelling and easy-to-understand manner.

What with the decline of mayfly hatches in some areas because of pesticide pollution, caddis flies, stone flies, and terrestrial insects are becoming more important to trout. This trend has resulted in a lot of dry-fly books over recent years. Several standouts are: *Hatches II*, Al Caucci and Bob Natasi; *Masters on the Dry Fly*, J. M. Migel and Dave Whitlock; *Meeting and Fishing the Hatches*, C. R. Meck; *Matching the Hatch*, Ernest Schwiebert; *A Modern Dry-Fly Code* and *In the Ring of the Rise*, Vincent Marinaro; *This Wonderful World of Trout* and *Rising Trout*, Charles K. Fox; *Fishing the Midge*, Ed Koch; *Tying and Fishing Terrestrials*, G. Almy; *Caddisflies*, Gary LaFontaine; *Stoneflies*, Swisher-Richards-Arbona; and *The Caddis and the Angler*, Solomon and Leiser. In *Fishing the Dry Fly as a Living Insect*, L. M.

Wright, Jr. suggests a new and deadly approach to fishing caddis flies—the "sudden inch" technique.

The following books do not fit the previous categories. But they deserve a niche in your angling library because they are landmarks of specialization and well written: Lee Wulff's great classic, *The Atlantic Salmon*; Leonard M. Wright, Jr.'s *Fly-Fishing Heresies*; and Dr. Donald DuBois's *Fisherman's Handbook of Trout Flies*, which contains descriptions of 5,939 fly patterns, excluding streamers. An ingenious cross-reference system enables you to discover a fly name by its description, or vice versa. *Stillwater Trout*, John Merwin, is required reading for those who fish for trout in lakes or reservoirs. I've found its advice useful when fishing beaver ponds in the Adirondacks. *Night Fishing for Trout*, H. James Bashline, is required reading for anyone searching for lunker trout. They often lose their inhibitions in darkness.

This potpourri of mixed categories would not be complete without mention of regional angling books. Among many are two standouts, because they center on the Catskills, "cradle of American fly fishing," and are superbly written by one of our premier angling writers and historians, Austin McK. Francis. His *Catskill Flytier* was co-authored by the late Harry Darbee, who—along with his wife, Elsie—was among the most beloved and gifted of fly-fishing personalities. Francis's *Catskill Rivers: Birthplace of American Fly Fishing* is the first major study of Catskill rivers and the anglers associated with them.

There are many fine literary works in a general vein. Several are recommended by critics as modern classics.

*The Gordon Garland*, an anthology by various angling writers; *A Fly Fisher's Life*, Charles Ritz; *The Well Tempered Angler*, Arnold Gingrich; *A River Never Sleeps*, Roderick

Haig-Brown; *Fishless Days, Angling Nights,* Sparse Grey Hackle; *The Complete Fly Fisherman — The Complete Notes and Letters of Theodore Gordon* and *Quill Gordon,* John MacDonald; *A River Runs Through It and Other Stories,* Norman Maclean; *The Part I Remember,* Charles Waterman; *The Year of the Angler,* Steve Raymond.

A monumental classic of modern times is Ernest G. Schwiebert's *Trout.* The last word on the prince of gamefish, this two-volume work is immense in scope but always interesting, thanks to the author's well-written prose. Bedside reading of the highest order — a longtime favorite of mine — is Schwiebert's *Remembrances of Rivers Past.*

Then there are the older classics. Some are hard to find. The larger libraries and the stores that sell second-hand books will have to be resorted to, along with houses that deal in rare books (e.g. The Anglers' and Shooters' Bookshelf). Walton's *Compleat Angler,* because of its many reprintings, is readily available. You will probably want to read such superb English literature as *The History of Fly Fishing for Trout* by John Waller Hills, Viscount Grey's *Fly Fishing,* Halford's *Dry Fly Fishing in Theory and Practice,* and G. E. M. Skues's *The Way of a Trout with a Fly,* plus the great American works by Edward Ringwood Hewitt, *A Trout and Salmon Fisherman for Seventy-five Years,* and *The Dry Fly and Fast Water* by George E. M. LaBranche.

In time, you may want to join a trout conservation group. My favorite is The Federation of Fly Fishers, P.O. Box 1088, West Yellowstone, Montana 59758, (406) 646-9541, because it espouses fly fishing as a conservation tool. While Trout Unlimited, 501 Church Street, N.E., Vienna, Virginia 22180, works for clean waters, it's not restricted to fly fishers. These organizations — and their regional affiliates — enable you to meet and get to know the country's leading fly anglers, who will be pleased to know you, too. For the stronger the membership of such bodies, the more effective will be their valuable work in furthering stream protection, regulation, and reclamation.

Your library won't be complete without a good fishing encyclopedia. A most thoroughly prepared one is *McClane's Standard Fishing Encyclopedia* by A. J. McClane.

There are numerous books on various aspects of sea fishing with flies, but I have confined myself here to only two: one general in nature, the other dwelling on a particularly popular branch of the sport. *Fly Fishing in Salt Water*, Lefty Kreh, covers a wide range of fish and techniques. *Fishing the Flats*, Mark Sosin and Lefty Kreh, concentrates on the exciting sport of bonefishing, along with the seeking of other sportfish of tidal flats.

Many fly anglers consider fly fishing and fly tying separate and distinct pastimes. In reality, of course, they are complementary. I maintain that you can't enjoy either to the optimum without being a practitioner of the other as well. So you should take up fly tying as soon as possible. A few books I've already recommended contain some fly-tying data, but this segment of the sport has become a genre unto itself. There are that many books! Forgive me for offering one of mine as a starter: *Tie a Fly; Catch a Trout*. George Harvey, the world renowned fly tier, was my collaborator.

The outdoor magazines can be valuable in providing angling know-how and where-to-go information. By the fire of a winter evening, their potential for vicarious kicks is great. Sometimes they contain classics. My initial interest in trout fishing as a boy arose from my reading of Ernest Hemingway's *Big Two-Hearted River*. My active involvement in trout conservation work resulted from an article in *Field & Stream* by Corey Ford, "I'll Fish Again Yesterday." Its bittersweet imagery drives home the need for wild rivers better than anything else I've ever read.

The deeper you delve into angling literature, the more you'll savor each day on a stream and the greater will be your anticipation of the next. The more you learn about trout fishing, the more you want to learn. In this sense, you will never be "the compleat angler," and herein lies the glory of the pastime. Though you may succeed admirably in thinking like a fish, the nature of things guarantees against perfecting the process. Over the years, though, you'll find yourself driven to try harder. Each experience will bring its own thrills and memories. None, however, will match the intensity of the one that made the later ones possible — the thrill of taking your first fish on a fly.

# Index